2021
EVANGEL
GATHERING

2021
Evangel
Gathering

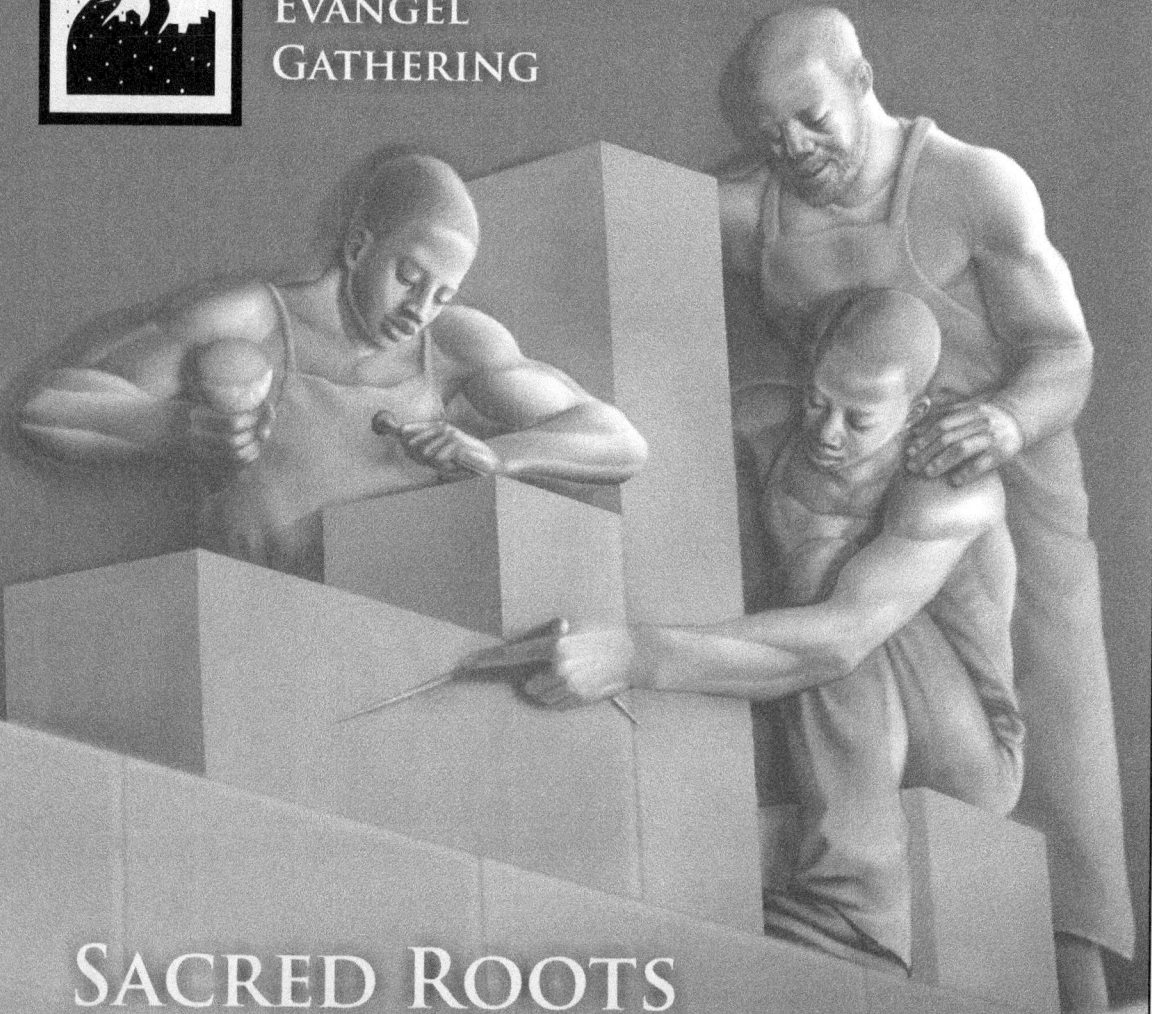

Sacred Roots
Thriving in Ministry

Apprenticed by the Early Church

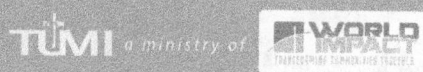

TUMI *a ministry of* WORLD IMPACT

TUMI Press • 3701 East 13th Street North • Suite 100 • Wichita, Kansas 67208

Table of Contents

Appendix

Welcome

Greetings, dear friends and fellow warriors, in the strong name of Jesus Christ!

Welcome to the *Sacred Roots Thriving in Ministry, Apprenticed by the Early Church* Evangel Gathering! We are excited about our partnership with Taylor University, Dr. Hank Voss and his colleagues, and with you to introduce a new generation to the wisdom and refreshment of the spiritual classics. Actually, we are not merely introducing you to classic works, but to leaders, church planters, bishops, Christian workers, mystics, poets, and excellent communicators of our faith. They were able to maneuver through tough times, weird doctrines, fierce persecution, and mind-numbing philosophies. In spite of it all, they came through with clarity, excellence, and grace, and provided us with insight and wisdom into powerful issues. Moreover, these men and women provided us with a pattern we can follow to see what it means to be both tenderhearted and tough minded, both of which are exhorted for our spiritual walk.

Your participation in this conference signals to you our confidence and gratitude for attending this event. We want the ancients to train us, to bless us, to guide us, and to equip us to live faithfully in the midst of a crooked generation and troubled hour. We hope to inspire you to open your heart to being equipped by the formers of the faith, men and women whose spiritual depth and intellectual gifts can be embraced by all of us, and enrich every dimension of our discipleship in Christ. Your position and maturity make you a prime candidate to walk others through this journey of apprenticeship and learning, of spirituality and faith.

We provide the presentations, dialogues, and resources of this conference for a single, dedicated purpose: to inspire you concerning the depth and richness of the ancient shapers of our spirituality and faith. If we form new relationships with them, and humbly listen to and learn from them, they can become our masters, training and equipping us in the insights and practices that forged a Christian generation that has given us our faith and generated our spiritual formation practices. It is a blessing to have you with us.

Welcome to the event. May God enrich our hearts as we humbly learn from the masters of our faith, those men and women who can equip us for a more fruitful life and ministry!

Under the tutelage of the ancients,

Rev. Dr. Don Davis

Speaker Biographies

Rev. Dr. Don Davis

Dr. Don Davis, founder and director of The Urban Ministry Institute, has been involved in urban ministry and missions with World Impact since 1975. He has spent his entire ministry career seeking to raise up a new generation of qualified spiritual leaders, pastors, and church planters who can build up Christ's Church in the most vulnerable and unreached urban communities in America and across the world. He is a graduate of Wheaton College (BA, Biblical Studies) and Wheaton Graduate School (MA, Systematic Theology,) with summa cum laude honors in both degrees. He earned his PhD in Religion (2000, Theology and Ethics) from the University of Iowa School of Religion. A recipient of numerous teaching and academic awards, he has also authored a number of books, curricula, and study materials all to equip, empower, and release biblical leaders to serve the Church of Jesus among the poor and oppressed, and display Kingdom transformation where they live and minister. He married his wife, Beth in February 1975, and together they have three children (one deceased), and four grandchildren.

Rev. Dr. Andrew Draper

Rev. Dr. Andrew T. Draper is the founding senior pastor of Urban Light Community Church. He is committed to a ministry of reconciliation, justice, and community development. Dr. Draper is actively involved in preaching, teaching, discipleship, education, and community advocacy. He is a sought-after speaker and conference presenter and has authored numerous books and articles on race, disability, and the church. Dr. Draper holds a PhD in theological ethics from the University of Aberdeen and a Master of Divinity from Winebrenner Theological Seminary.

Rev. Bob Engel

Bob joined The Urban Ministry Institute in October 2016, serving as the National Church Planting Director. He serves to assess, resource, and coordinate urban cross-cultural church planters and their efforts on behalf of World Impact's missionaries, urban church plant teams, and other missional partners who are seeking to plant healthy, reproducing churches and facilitate church plant movements among America's urban poor. Bob and his wife, Susan, have four children: Rachel, Tristan, Chase, and Mihaly.

Dr. Carmen Joy Imes

Carmen Joy Imes (PhD, Wheaton College) is Associate Professor of Old Testament at Prairie College in Three Hills, Alberta. She and her husband served as missionaries with SIM for fifteen years. Carmen is the author of *Bearing God's Name: Why Sinai Still Matters* (IVP 2019) and blogs at *carmenjoyimes.blogspot.com*.

Rev. Dr. Kwesi Kamau

Rev. Dr. Kwesi Kamau is an author, activist theologian, and serves as the Lead Pastor of IMPACT Church in Dallas, Texas. His writing, speaking, preaching, and teaching have served to inspire thousands to live their best lives in service to God and humanity. Dr. Kamau also leads Impact Discipleship, LLC, to empower churches to comprehensively transform their communities from the inside out through prayer and discipleship. He has written several books, including *A Passion for Prayer and Better Days: Encouragements for Every Day*. First and foremost a family man, Dr. Kamau is grateful to share his life and ministry with his wife, Monti, their five fantastic children—Nia, Jada, Bailey, Josiah, and Jeremiah, and his mother, Ann Bailey.

Rev. Eric Himelick

Eric and Rachelle Himelick are currently serving as the Director of Urban Ministry and Development for Evangelistic Faith Missions. They live with their six children— Kaylynn, Rebecca, Sarah, Samuel, Esther, and Karissa—in Upland, Indiana, at Victory Acres Farm. Eric graduated in 2000 from Union Bible College with a degree in Pastoral Ministry. Rachelle attended UBC for two years. They served as the founding directors of Victory Inner-City Ministries for fifteen years before joining EFM in June 2015.

Rev. Dr. Greg Peters

Greg Peters is Professor of Medieval and Spiritual Theology at Biola University. He is also the Servants of Christ Research Professor of Monastic Studies and Ascetical Theology at Nashotah House Theological Seminary and Rector at Anglican Church of the Epiphany, La Mirada, California.

Rev. Dr. Hank Voss

Hank Voss is assistant professor of Christian Ministry at Taylor University. He has authored, co-authored, or edited twelve books including *Introduction to Evangelical Theology* (T&T Clark, 2021) and *The Priesthood of All Believers and the* Missio Dei (2016). He serves as Senior National Staff with The Urban Ministry Institute (TUMI), and directs the Lilly-funded Sacred Roots Thriving in Ministry Project for which he is currently editing Aelred of Rievaulx's (d. 1167) classic, *Spiritual Friendship* (SRSC 3). Hank, his wife Johanna, and their four teenage children reside in Muncie, Indiana.

PLENARIES

The Need for Apprenticeship:
Biblical Foundations for the Pursuit of Wise Spiritual Mentors

Rev. Dr. Don L. Davis

> A disciple is not above his teacher, but everyone when he is fully trained will be like his teacher.
>
> ~ Jesus, Luke 6.40 (ESV)
>
> Seeker: a person or thing that seeks
>
> ~ dictionary.com, https://www.dictionary.com/browse/seeker?s=t
>
> Sensei: (can be pronounced "Sensai" as well), *Sinsang, Sonsaeng, Seonsaeng* or *Xiansheng* is an honorific term shared in Chinese honorifics and Japanese honorifics that is translated as "person born before another" or "one who comes before."
>
> ~ Wikipedia
> https://en.wikipedia.org/wiki/Sensei

I. **The *Paradigm* of Apprenticeships: Movements, Leaders, and Apprenticeships**

2 Thess. 2.15 (ESV) – So then, brothers, stand firm and hold to the traditions that you were taught by us, either by our spoken word or by our letter.

A. The Golden Strand: How do movements among the underserved start, grow, and thrive?

1. *Strand one*: The role of the founder: Moses

2. *Strand two*: The synergy of the "first followers:" Joshua

3. *Strand three*: The strength of young apprentices in a tradition: Jehu, Gideon, Samson, Samuel

4. The power of tradition: not a dirty word

   a. *Paradosis*: the handing down to another the invaluable deposit

   b. A mixture of content and loyalty

   c. Traditioned innovation (Dr. Alvin Sanders): building on the legacy given, engaging on the situation encountered

B. Why apprenticeships work: a strategic methodology to equip movements in communities of poverty

   1. They are *organic*: receiving protection, care, and training from another.

   2. They are *affordable*: they require presence not funds.

   3. They are *transparent*: you learn on the job in the presence of a valid leader.

   4. They are *reliable*: authority is given after verified loyalty and service.

   5. They are *reproducible*: once a system of apprenticeship is begun, it can be replicated indefinitely.

C. The biblical blueprint of a worthy apprenticeship

    1. The *call of God*: a publicly acknowledged and confirmed call

    2. The *character of Christ*: proven character in the midst of lived life

    3. The *charisma of the Holy Spirit*: anointing and gifting in the church

    4. The *connection to the church community*: compelling testimony within and among the people of the body

D. Biblical examples of mentoring and apprenticeship

    1. Moses and Joshua (Num. 27.15-20, cf. Josh. 1.1-2)

    2. Elijah and Elisha (1 Kings 19; 2 Kings 2)

    3. David and his "mighty men" (1 Chron. 12)

    4. Naomi and Ruth (Ruth 1)

    5. Jesus and the Twelve (Mark 3.14)

    6. Paul and Timothy (and his band), (Acts 20.4 cf. Phil.2.20-22)

    7. Aquila and Priscilla alongside Apollos (Acts 18.26)

II. The *Profitability* of Being Apprenticed by the Ancients in the Spiritual Classics

> **Why Should Leaders in Movements of Communities of Poverty Become the Apprentices Under the Ancients' Tutelage?**
>
> Psalm 78.1-4 (ESV) 1 Give ear, O my people, to my teaching; incline your ears to the words of my mouth! [2] I will open my mouth in a parable; I will utter dark sayings from of old, [3] things that we have heard and known, that our fathers have told us. [4] We will not hide them from their children, but tell to the coming generation the glorious deeds of the LORD, and his might, and the wonders that he has done.

  A. *History*: We see how they shaped the truths of the one true Faith we now defend.

    1. Close to apostolic age

    2. Embroiled in defending the faith in the midst of "pagan" neighbors

    3. Imagination in conceiving how to move forward in conversations with those detractors inside and outside the church

  B. *Strategy*: We watch how "the best of us" dealt with similar attitudes, situations, and problems we face and encounter today.

    1. Pick up tips in approaching tough questions and conflicts.

    2. Gain insight in wrestling with problems affecting the Faith.

    3. Learn how to address seemingly unresolvable issues with biblical creativity.

C. *Empathy*: We become friends with some of our deepest saints in times gone by.

   1. We sit at their feet and learn from their actions (and mistakes).

   2. We appreciate their "fierce tenderness" in engaging difficult conversations.

   3. We gain a better perspective of the context of the Early Church, our ancestors in Christ.

D. *Inspiration*: We gain insights from their experience and reflection that point to new ways of thinking, worldview, and problem solving.

   1. Their experience was powerful and moving.

   2. They provide unique answers to really difficult questions.

   3. They drill down to the bone on issues rarely discussed thoroughly today.

E. *Reflection*: We gain new language, concepts, and perspectives that enrich and challenge our understanding of our spiritual walk and mission.

   1. We discover new ways to say the same things.

   2. We see that the ancients did not claim to have or actually had all the answers.

   3. They provide perspective (new points of view) to see and discuss old issues.

F. *Delight*: We are satisfied as we explore what it means to live faithfully.

1. We will grow in our love for Christ.

2. We will admire our spiritual "stock."

3. We will experience real satisfaction in the ways they addressed the connection of the Faith and our lives together.

III. The *Principle* of Apprenticeship: Leadership as Representation (*The Role of Fomal Proxy: Leadership as Representation*)

John 8.31-32 (ESV) – So Jesus said to the Jews who had believed him, "If you abide in my word, you are truly my disciples, [32] and you will know the truth, and the truth will set you free."

A. Apostles, evangelists, prophets, and ambassadors: representatives of another

B. Jesus as the perfect pattern of the representative of God

C. The dynamics of representation

1. The *Commissioning*: formal selection and call

2. The *Equipping*: appropriate training and investment

3. The *Entrustment*: endowed with the authority and power to act on behalf of the movement

4. The *Mission*: faithful execution of the task

5. The *Reckoning*: assessment and evaluation of the results attained

6. The *Reward*: recognition and reward based on the faithful service and results attained

D. The Dialogue of Representation

> Ongoing dialogue and critical conversation with their teachers over the essentials is the primary way the apprenticed gain skill and expertise in making the tradition come alive in the midst of the community.

1. *Clarity of our essential core*: Knowing precisely who we are and what it means

2. *Dialogical interaction in connection to scenarios*: Constant engagement in case study assessment: how does the core apply to this situation

3. *Situational re-application of truths gained for new circumstances*: applying new insights of our tradition to our living and changing situation

IV. The *Process* of Apprenticeships: From Seeker to Sensei (Steps to Equipping Others)

> Psalm 71.18 (ESV) – So even to old age and gray hairs, O God, do not forsake me, until I proclaim your might to another generation, your power to all those to come.

A. *Join us!*: Adopt the movement and commit to represent its identity, purpose, and mission.

B. *Become an apprentice of the Ancients yourself*: Distinguish yourself in the movement as a champion of faithfulness of service.

C. *Find new students to engage together*: Receive apprentices for future representation and authority in the movement.

D. *Build new relationships of mentoring and friendship*: Instruct and model movement representation task in the presence of and accompanied by the apprentices.

E. *Pass the baton*: Co-labor in movement representation as colleagues and comrades together.

F. *Let them fly*: Give the apprentice solo assignments, with you only accompanying as support.

G. *Dub them your equal*: Assign the apprentice formal leadership status, i.e., to take on their own apprenticeships as agent of the movement.

V. The *Problems* of Apprenticeships: the Rough Edges of Apprenticeship

Jude 1.3 (ESV) – Beloved, although I was very eager to write to you about our common salvation, I found it necessary to write appealing to you to contend for the faith that was once for all delivered to the saints.

A. *Movement creep*: Unclear as to what the movement is, stands for, or seeks to do

B. *Secret society*: No discernible path to join or align with our movement

C. *Unspoken pathways*: Neglect of specific ways movement folk can engage and represent the movement, whatever the level

D. *Phony channels of opportunity*: tolerating unhealthy folk or promoting folk with unproven track records among us

E. *No recognition or promotion*: failing to reward loyalty and service

VI. The *Practice* of Apprenticeships: Take-aways for a New Vision

> Hebrews 13.7-8 (ESV) – Remember your leaders, those who spoke to you the word of God. Consider the outcome of their way of life, and imitate their faith. [8] Jesus Christ is the same yesterday and today and forever.

A. Clarify your movement play-book: Who, what, why, how . . .

B. Make the invitation: boldly, clearly, and often.

C. Ask God for insight into your choice of the next generation of leaders.

D. Offer specific roles, assignments for the most loyal "first followers."

E. Develop a workable, modest apprenticeship program, focused on investment.

F. Provide both oversight, provision, and answerability throughout the entire period.

G. Certify your apprentices: Be ready to delegate the assignments and authority once the program is successfully completed.

Closing quotes from Sensei Mr. Miyagi

"Either you karate do 'yes' or karate do 'no.' You karate do 'guess so,' (get squished) just like grape."

The point: Once you commit to an enterprise, do it with your full heart and effort. Or not, and pay the price.

"Never trust a spiritual leader who cannot dance."

The point: Every true leader has to be flexible, adaptable, and able to enjoy themselves in the process. Correction and celebration!

Notes

The Cost of Apprenticeship:
Historical Foundations for the Pursuit of Wise Spiritual Mentors

Rev. Dr. Kwesi Kamau

I. Introduction: Historical Models for Historic Moments

A. The case of Ephesus: generational drift

1. A full-blown, world-changing movement

2. "Forsaking your first love"

3. Generational drift

B. The gift of remembering

1. Yields practical wisdom

2. Inspires courage and endurance

3. Connects with bigger story

II. John Wesley: From Roots to Fruits

A. A powerful movement

1. Global outreach: Britain and America

    2. Social impact: slavery, democracy, social responsibility

    3. Reasonable enthusiasm: qualifying experience

  B. A powerful method

    1. Deepening disciples: heart to hear experiences

    2. Training leaders: women and men, rich and poor

  C. Powerful administration

    1. Societies (preach houses), class meetings, bands

    2. Itinerate preachers: districts and conferences

III. John Wesley: *A Christian Library*

  A. Wesley's personal experience

  B. Wesley's *A Christian Library*

    1. Purpose and description

    2. Success or failure?

IV. Lessons from *A Christian Library*

A. Proper context

B. Proper readings

C. Proper discipline

Notes

Mere Missions:
Keep Moving Forward

Rev. Bob Engel

I. War of the Worlds: The Big Picture

A. Purpose

1. The Kingdom of Darkness

   a. To rule and reign

   b. To be worshipped

2. The Kingdom of God

   a. To rule and reign

   b. To be worshipped

B. Priority

1. The Kingdom of Darkness

   a. Souls

   b. Bondage, division, and foul play

    2. The Kingdom of God

        a. Souls

        b. Freedom, wholeness, and justice

  C. Plan (for souls)

    1. The Kingdom of Darkness

        a. Silence the Gospel – Jesus.

        b. Servants of unrighteousness

    2. The Kingdom of God

        a. Proclaim the Gospel – Jesus.

        b. Servants of righteousness

II. The Campaign: M3

  A. Missions

    1. Jesus is Lord of missions.

        a. The mandate to "go"

        b. The promise of presence

    2. Evangel

        a. Evangel's missions planks

        b. Evangel's missions platform

B. Movements

    1. Jesus is Lord of movements.

        a. The complexity and vastness of the harvest field

        b. The wisdom of movements

    2. Evangel

        a. Strategic commitments

        b. Standard practices

C. Multiplication

    1. Jesus is Lord of multiplication.

        a. The wisdom of multiplication

        b. The means of multiplication

2. Evangel

    a. Catalyzing leaders of church planting movements

    b. D.S.A.

III. Keep Moving Forward.

A. HOW

    1. Endearment

        a. The Lord Jesus

        b. Intel: Our Sacred Roots

    2. Endure

        a. Not of those who shrink back

        b. To the very end

B. WHAT

    1. Evangel

        a. Joint operations: The Allied Forces

        b. Apprenticeships

2. SRTM Initiative

   a. Your strategic plan

   b. Spiritual Classics

C. WHY

1. Determination of God

   a. To call out and to gather

   b. Populate his Kingdom.

2. The famous final scene

   a. The end is inevitable.

   b. The end is near.

Notes

SMALL GROUPS
& NETWORKING

Introductions

Notes on Small Group Members

Presenting Cohort Plans

I. Sharing of Highlights and Lowlights from Conference So Far (10 min)

II. What still needs clarity? (10 min)

1. Questions?

2. Comments?

3. Concerns?

III. Overview of How to Present Your Action Plan (5 min)

1. 2 minutes to describe your cohort

2. 1 minute to describe the model of meeting your group will use

3. 1 minute to name four key dates for your action plan

4. 2 minutes to describe the order of spiritual mentors your group will pursue in 2021-2022 and why

5. 2 minutes for questions, comments, and encouragement

IV. Personal Prep (5 min)

V. Small Group Members Present Thrive Plans (50 min)

A. Member #1 Presents Thrive Plan

B. Member #2 Presents Thrive Plan

C. Member #3 Presents Thrive Plan

D. Member #4 Presents Thrive Plan

E. Member #5 Presents Thrive Plan

VI. Encouragement and Close (10 min)

Small Group Prayer

Small Group Prayer Requests

Break and Networking Opportunity

Networking Notes

WORKSHOPS

"Means": How to Lead a Sacred Roots Cohort

Rev. Eric Himelick and Rev. Dr. Hank Voss

> It has always therefore been one of my main endeavors as a teacher to persuade the young that firsthand knowledge is not only more worth acquiring than second-hand knowledge, but is usually much easier and more delightful to acquire. . . . It is a good rule, after reading a new book, never to allow yourself another new one till you have read an old one in between. If that is too much for you, you should at least read one old one to every three new ones.
>
> ~ C. S. Lewis, 1944
>
> You should read twenty-five percent of your books from the first 1,500 years of church history, twenty-five percent from the last 500 years, twenty-five percent from the last 100 years, and twenty-five percent from recent years.
>
> ~ Rick Warren, 2010

I. Introduction: The Sacred Roots Origin Story

II. Apprenticing Ourselves to Mighty Mentors by Reading Spiritual Classics

    A. Apprenticeship principles for reading spiritual classics

        1. Lessons learned at Englewood Christian Church[1]

        2. Lessons learned from James Houston[2]

---

1 C. Christopher Smith, *Reading for the Common Good: How Books Help Our Churches and Neighborhoods Flourish* (Downers Grove, IL: Intervarsity, 2016).

2 James Houston, "A Guide to Devotional Reading," in *The Love of God*, Reprint (1983), Classics of Faith and Devotion (Vancouver, British Columbia: Regent College, 2018), 253–260.

B. Apprenticeship and three kinds of mentors

> Apprenticeship provides a system for training a new generation of practitioners in a trade or profession with on-the-job training and often includes accompanying study (cohort work and reading).

1. **Mentor (Ancient).** Every generation of the Church has produced gifted leaders, but some leaders have influenced not only their own generation, but every generation that has come after them. Christian leaders have continued to find these wise practitioners to be helpful mentors for soul work and soul care across many generations.

2. **Mentor (Contemporary).** Sacred Roots Contemporary Mentors are world-class evangelical scholars who have spent years getting to know the Ancient Mentors we meet in the *Sacred Roots Spiritual Classics*. Each Contemporary Mentor has edited one volume in the *Sacred Roots Spiritual Classics* series and produced a number of resource videos to help contemporary church leaders apprentice themselves to the ancient mentors of the Church.

3. **Mentor (Local).** Sacred Roots Local Mentors are the leaders of specific groups of congregational leaders who have gathered in a cohort to learn from an Ancient Mentor like Augustine, Benedict, Basil, and others. Local Mentors know the context and the communities in which the cohort leaders work and they nurture and encourage friendships within the cohort they lead.

C. Apprenticeship practices: How to "read" a spiritual classic

1. Spiritual reading is different from other kinds of reading

a. Different from reading the Bible

      b.   Different from reading a textbook

      c.   Different from reading a novel

  2. Strategies for reading a spiritual classic

      a.   "Reading" with your ears (audio books)

      b.   Regular reading (time and place)

      c.   Reading on the Sabbath

III. The Art of Friendship: How to Build Friendships with Spiritual Classics

> Make friendship a fine art.
>
> ~ John Wooden

A. Three kinds of spiritual friends

  1. Friends in the "cloud" (Hebrews 12:1–2)

      a.   The authors of the spiritual classics

      b.   Sisters and brothers from past generations who have read the spiritual classics before us

          (1) Augustine was powerfully impacted by a spiritual classic written by Athanasius called *The Life of St. Anthony*.[3]

---

3   David Wright, "The Life Changing 'Life of Antony,'" *Christian History Institute* (blog), 1999, https://christianhistoryinstitute.org/magazine/article/life-changing-life-of-antony.

(2) The Baptist pastor Charles Spurgeon read John Bunyan's *Pilgrim's Progress* more than one hundred times.

(3) Pheobe Palmer, D.L. Moody and Watchmen Nee had their vision for prayer deeply shaped by a spiritual classic by Jeanne-Marie Guyon entitled *A Short and Very Easy Method of Prayer*.[4]

2. Friends in this generation

    a. Spiritual friends in my Jerusalem (my city)

    b. Spiritual friends in my Judea and Samaria (my region)

    c. Spiritual friends at the ends of the earth (global Church)

3. Friends in my cohort

    a. Spiritual friends in my fellowship

    b. Art friends (spiritual friends with whom I pursue the fine art of friendship)

---

4   Glen G. Scorgie, "The Diffusion of Christian Mysticism: From the Medieval Rhineland to Contemporary China," *Spiritus: A Journal of Christian Spirituality 20*, no. 1 (2020): 1–24.

B. Three models for reading *Sacred Roots Spiritual Classics* together

1. Weekly strategy for engaging spiritual classics

SRSC Section to Read	"Sunday School" Class	"Church-Based Seminary" Model
	Ten Weeks	Eight Weeks
Introduction	Week 1	Week 1
Chapter 1	Week 2	
Chapter 2	Week 3	Week 2
Chapter 3	Week 4	Week 3
Chapter 4	Week 5	Week 4
Chapter 5	Week 6	Week 5
Chapter 6	Week 7	Week 6
Chapter 7	Week 8	Week 7
Chapter 8	Week 9	Week 8
Continuing the Conversation	Week 10	

a. Sample weekly cohort meeting

b. Things to remember

2. Monthly strategy for engaging spiritual classics

a. Sample monthly cohort meeting

SRSC Section to Read	Monthly Pastor's Meeting
Introduction	Month 1
Chapter 1	
Chapter 2	
Chapter 3	Month 2
Chapter 4	
Chapter 5	
Chapter 6	
Chapter 7	Month 3
Chapter 8	
Continuing the Conversation	

b. Things to remember

3. Quarterly strategy for engaging spiritual classics

    a. Sample quarterly cohort meeting

SRSC Section to Read	Quarterly Retreat Discussion Group
	Quarterly
Introduction	
Chapter 1	
Chapter 2	
Chapter 3	
Chapter 4	Read text before retreat and then discuss.
Chapter 5	
Chapter 6	
Chapter 7	
Chapter 8	
Continuing the Conversation	

    b. Things to remember

IV. Three Strategies for Engaging Spiritual Classics with Spiritual Friends

A. Strategy #1: Ask good questions to one another.

1. Jesus was a master at asking questions. He asks well over 300 questions in the Gospels.[5]

2. Every chapter in a *Sacred Roots Spiritual Classic* includes five kinds of questions to encourage reflection and conversation. You are the expert on your context, so do not limit yourself to these questions. If there are others that fit better use them. The five kinds of questions in *Sacred Roots Spiritual Classics* include questions about our habitat, our heads, our hearts, our hands, and our habits.

Habitat? Habitat questions ask us to pause and look around at our environment, our culture, our generation, our nationality, and the things that make up the *Zeitgeist* (spirit of the times). Questions may ask about the author's habitat or our own. Since the *SRSC* were written across many centuries and cultures, they often help us notice aspects of our culture needing attention.

Head? Auguste Rodin's sculpture known as *The Thinker* sits before an 18-foot-tall sculpture called *The Gates of Hell.* The massive sculptural group reflects Rodin's engagement with a spiritual classic by Dante, *The Divine Comedy. Head questions* require serious intellectual engagement as you talk with friends about the author's ideas, claims, and proposals.

Heart? In August of 1541 John Calvin wrote a letter to a friend with this promise: "When I remember that I am not my own, I offer up my heart presented as a sacrifice to God." Calvin's personal seal expressed this sincere desire. God not only owns our mind, but also our will and emotions. *Heart questions* will help you attend to the people and things to which you give your loves.

---

5   Martin B. Copenhaver, *Jesus Is the Question: The 307 Questions Jesus Asked and the 3 He Answered* (Nashville: Abingdon, 2014).

Hands? Albrecht Dürer sketched a drawing called *Study of the Hands of an Apostle* in the year 1508. The apostles were men of action, yet Dürer portrays the apostle's hands in prayer. The action to which *SRSC* call us are often surprising. *Hands questions* will challenge you to evaluate carefully what action you are to take after a particular reading.

Habits? Charlotte Mason (d. 1923) was a master teacher. She believed Christian formation must carefully attend to habit formation. Like laying railroad tracks, habit formation is hard work. But once laid, great work requires little effort just as railroad cars run smoothly on tracks. *Habit questions* challenge you to reflect on small daily or weekly actions that form your character and the character of those around you.

B. Strategy #2: Take advantage of expert testimony to spark conversation.

    1. Use the Sacred Roots discussion videos.

        a. Every spiritual classic in the *Sacred Roots Series* has ten short videos available to stimulate engagement and conversation with a particular spiritual classic.

        b. Each video includes the "Five H" discussion questions from the chapter being discussed.

    2. Check for other video resources for additional background on particular spiritual classics.

C. Strategy #3: Engage the spiritual classics with both audio and visual strategies.

1. Enjoy the artwork in the spiritual classics.

2. Take advantage of the audio book versions.

V. Why Won't This Work?

A. Be aware of the opposition from our flesh (internal).

B. Be aware of the opposition from the world (external)

C. Be aware of the devil's opposition (infernal).

"Means": Forming Your Cohort Plan Using Sacred Roots Spiritual Classics

Rev. Eric Himelick and Rev. Dr. Hank Voss

> No one presumes to teach an art until he has first carefully studied it. Look how foolish it is for the inexperienced to assume pastoral authority, since the care of souls is the art of arts!
>
> ~ Gregory the Great, c. 590
>
> Your leaders . . . keep watch over your souls and will give an account for their work.
>
> ~ Hebrews 13:17a

I. Meet our Mentors: Augustine, Basil, Aelred, and Thurman (plus others!)

A. Dr. Carmen Imes, Augustine, and Friends

> Notes on Ancient and Contemporary Mentors for This Volume

B. Rev. Dr. Greg Peters, Basil, and Benedict

> Notes on Ancient and Contemporary Mentors for This Volume

C. Rev. Dr. Hank Voss, Aelred, and Friends

> Notes on Ancient and Contemporary Mentors for This Volume

D. Rev. Dr. Andrew Draper, Howard Thurman, and Friends

> Notes on Ancient and Contemporary Mentors for This Volume

E. What kind of mentors do my leaders need to meet?

> The Ancient Mentor the leaders in my cohort will find most interesting will be . . .

II. Soul Work and Soul Care Overview for Volumes 1–4

Soul Work. "Soul work" is the personal work of watering, weeding, pruning, and fertilizing the garden of one's own soul. Jesus often used metaphors from the medical and agricultural professions when describing this "soul work" to which he called his disciples.

Soul Care. Soul care is the pastoral work of nurturing growth in another's friendship with God. Like a doctor for souls, or a farmer caring for an orchard of fruit trees, congregational leaders can learn much about caring for souls by apprenticing ourselves to the wisdom of the great doctors of the church from previous generations.

A. SRSC Vol. 1 – Soul Work and Soul Care with Augustine as mentor

> What kind of soul work engagement and soul care practices will this volume help my leaders develop?

B. SRSC Vol. 2 – Soul Work and Soul Care with Benedict and Basil as mentors

> What kind of soul work engagement and soul care practices will this volume help my leaders develop?

C. SRSC Vol 3 – Soul Work and Soul Care with Aelred as mentor

> What kind of soul work engagement and soul care practices will this volume help my leaders develop?

D. SRSC Vol 4 – Soul Work and Soul Care with Thurman and Others as Mentors

> What kind of soul work engagement and soul care practices will this volume help my leaders develop?

III. In What Order Should Our Cohort Read the SRSCs?

A. Option 1: The Sacred Roots subject area published order

B. Option 2: A contextualized and/or personally prioritized order

IV. Putting Our Cohort Thrive Plan Together

A. Leadership

1. Cohort local mentor

2. Cohort "Timothy"

B. Membership

1. Who are the leaders that will be invited to participate?

2. What criteria will be used?

C. Model for meeting

1. Which model will our cohort be using?

2. What adaptations will I need to make due to my context?

D. Moses's Hierarchy of Needs (Not Maslow's)

1. What spiritual classics will best get the discussions going?

2. What spiritual classics address soul work or soul care issues most needed by my cohort?

3. In what order will we read and discuss the spiritual classics this year?

V. Reward, Recognition, and Resources for Our Cohort Teams

A. The reward of greater endearment to Christ

B. The reward of a richer embrace of one another

C. Further opportunities for spiritual evaluation and recognition of growth

   1. Personal or cohort participation in The Christian Life Assessment[1]

   2. For Sacred Roots Evangel Gathering 2021-2022 cohort members

      a. Use the Google form to report progress after completing discussing your first spiritual classic as a cohort.

      b. The Sacred Roots Project will send you copies of the Abide Bible, a Bible with over 1,000 Scripture Engagement activities in it, for each member of your cohort.

---

1   Available for free to Sacred Roots participants at *https://www.taylor.edu/center-for-scripture-engagement/survey/index.shtml.*

APPENDIX

APPENDIX 1

Cohort Thrive Plan

A Sacred Roots Thrive Plan is a way to thrive, not simply survive in ministry. A thrive plan is the specific intentional strategy a cohort adopts to apprentice together under a master practitioner of life with God. (Augustine, Athanasius, Benedict, Basil, etc.).

Movement Name: _____

Cohort Leader: _____   **Cohort "Timothy":** _____

Member Names: _____   _____

_____   _____

_____   _____

_____   _____

Model for Meeting *(Any modifications or special notes)*

	Apprenticeship Order	Soul Work/Soul Skill Focus
1		
2		
3		
4		

Key Dates

1 First Cohort Meeting with Vol 1: _____

2 First Cohort Meeting with Vol 2: _____

3 First Cohort Meeting with Vol 3: _____

4 First Cohort Meeting with Vol 4: _____

5 Multiply Conference: May _____

APPENDIX 2

"Engage Scripture Like an Augustine?"

Wise mentors across church history have had powerful impact on their generation and many more because of their deep engagement with Scripture. Today, millions of global believers are apprenticing themselves to wise mentors and learning to practice Scripture Engagement. Below are some helpful descriptions of Scripture Engagement.

> Scripture engagement calls us to a cycle of study-reflection-study-reflection, which leads to a deepened relationship with God and a changed life, is the most powerful process for developing spiritually.
>
> ~ Dr. Phil Collins, Taylor University Center for Scripture Engagement, Editor of the Abide Bible

> Scripture engagement is interaction with the biblical text in a way that provides sufficient opportunity for the text to speak for itself by the power of the Holy Spirit, enabling readers and listeners to hear the voice of God and discover for themselves the unique claim Jesus Christ is making upon them.
>
> ~ Dr. Fergus Macdonald, Former Lausanne Executive Chair

> Bible engagement is the process whereby people are connected with the Bible such that they have meaningful encounters with Jesus Christ and their lives are progressively transformed in Him.
>
> ~ Dr. Lawson Murray, President Scripture Union Canada

> Facilitating life-changing encounters with God through His Word.
>
> ~ Wycliffe Asia-Pacific & SIL Asia Scripture Engagement Forum

> Scripture Engagement is "encountering God's Word in a life-changing way."
>
> ~ Forum of Bible Agencies International

To learn more about Scripture Engagement visit the many free resources at *www.biblegateway.com/resources/scripture-engagement/*

About the Sacred Roots Project

The Sacred Roots Thriving in Ministry Project seeks to equip and empower under-resourced congregational leaders in urban, rural, and incarcerated communities. One avenue for accomplishing this goal is the Sacred Roots Spiritual Classics, a series of abridged Christian spiritual classics that equip congregational leaders to engage the wealth of the Great Tradition.

The Sacred Roots Spiritual Classics are dedicated to all Christian leaders who have loved the poor and have recognized the importance of Christian spiritual classics for nurturing the next generation. We especially recognize these fourteen:

- John Wesley (1703–1791)
- Rebecca Protten (1718–1780)
- Elizabeth Fry (1780–1845)
- Phoebe Palmer (1807–1874)
- Dora Yu (1873–1931)
- A. W. Tozer (1897–1963)
- Howard Thurman (1899–1981)
- Watchman Nee (1903–1972)
- James Houston (1922–)
- J. I. Packer (1926–2020)
- Tom Oden (1931–2016)
- René Padilla (1932–)
- Dallas Willard (1935–2013)
- Bruce Demarest (1935–2021)

> Remember your leaders,
> those who spoke to you the word of God.
> Consider the outcome of their way of life,
> and imitate their faith.
>
> ~ Hebrews 13.7

APPENDIX 4

Glossary of Terms for Sacred Roots Evangel Gathering

1. **Scripture Engagement.** Scripture Engagement is the process whereby people are connected with the Bible such that they have meaningful encounters with Jesus Christ and their lives are progressively transformed through the power of the Holy Spirit.

2. **Soul Work.** "Soul work" is the personal work of watering, weeding, pruning, and fertilizing the garden of one's own soul. Jesus often used metaphors from the medical and agricultural professions when describing this "soul work" to which he called his disciples.

3. **Soul Care.** Soul care is the pastoral work of nurturing growth in another's friendship with God. Like a doctor for souls, or a farmer caring for an orchard of fruit trees, congregational leaders can learn much about caring for souls by apprenticing ourselves to the wisdom of the great doctors of the church from previous generations.

4. **Apprenticeship.** Apprenticeship provides a system for training a new generation of practitioners in a trade or profession with on-the-job training and often includes accompanying study (cohort work and reading).

5. **Cohort.** A cohort is a group of students who work through a curriculum together to achieve particular learning objectives together. Cohorts provide a richness to the learning process due to the multiple perspectives offered by the participants. A Sacred Roots Cohort consists of Congregational Leaders who are learning together under the guidance of a local mentor, a contemporary mentor, and an ancient mentor.

6. **Small Group (Conference).** At the 2021 Sacred Roots Evangel Gathering a small group consists of 4-6 church plant movement leaders who will each be leading a Sacred Roots Cohort during 2021-2022.

7. **P. W. R.** PWR is an abbreviation standing for Prepare. Work. Review. It is a model for developing wisdom as one engages in the important work of faithful and fruitful ministry.

8. **Spiritual Classic.** A spiritual classic is a non-canonical text that has proven helpful in addressing perennial pastoral problems (i.e. helpful for "curing souls") across many cultures and over many centuries.

9. **Sacred Roots Spiritual Classics.** The Sacred Roots Spiritual Classics (SRSC) are a collection of sixteen spiritual classics divided into four subject areas: Biblical Studies, Theology and Ethics, Christian Ministry, and Global Mission.

10. **Mentor (Ancient).** Every generation of the church has produced gifted leaders, but some leaders have influenced not only their own generation, but every generation that has come after them. Christian leaders have continued to find these wise practitioners to be helpful mentors for soul work and soul care across many generations.

11. **Mentor (Contemporary).** Sacred Roots Contemporary Mentors are world class evangelical scholars who have spent years getting to know the Ancient Mentors we meet in the Sacred Roots Spiritual Classics. Each Contemporary Mentor has edited one volume in the Sacred Roots Spiritual Classics series and produced a number of resource videos to help contemporary church leaders apprentice themselves to the ancient mentors of the church.

12. **Mentor (Local).** Sacred Roots Local Mentors are the leaders of specific groups of congregational leaders who have gathered in a cohort to learn from an Ancient Mentor like Augustine, Benedict, Basil, and others. Local Mentors know the context and the communities in which the cohort leaders work and they nurture and encourage friendships within the cohort they lead.

13. **Thrive Plan.** A Sacred Roots Thrive Plan is a way to thrive, not simply survive in ministry. A thrive plan is the specific intentional strategy a cohort adopts to apprentice together under a master practitioner of life with God (e.g. Augustine, Athanasius, Benedict, Basil, etc.).

14. **Spiritual formation.** Spiritual formation is a process empowered by the Holy Spirit where the inner person is conformed more and more to the inner person of Christ.

15. **Discipleship.** Conforming all areas of life to the Lordship of Jesus Christ with special attention to the relational, transformational, and vocational dimensions.

16. **Church Plant Movement.** A church plant movement or CPM is a movement of churches that are rapidly reproducing themselves as a normal aspect of their internal DNA.

17. **Five Es.** The Five Es refer to: Endear. Evangelism. Equip. Empower. Embrace. Each of these "Es" describes a specific task that church planters must consider intentionally in order to thrive personally and to plant churches that will bring kingdom transformation to our broken world.

Appendix 5

Ten Key Cross-Cultural Church Planting Principles

World Impact

1. **Jesus is Lord.** (Matt. 9.37-38) All church plant activity is made effective and fruitful under the watch care and power of the Lord Jesus, who himself is the Lord of the harvest.

2. **Evangelize, Equip, and Empower unreached people to reach people.** (1 Thess. 1.6-8) Our goal in reaching others for Christ is not only for solid conversion but also for dynamic multiplication; those who are reached must be trained to reach others as well.

3. **Be inclusive: whosoever will may come.** (Rom. 10.12) No strategy should forbid any person or group from entering into the Kingdom through Jesus Christ by faith.

4. **Be culturally neutral: Come just as you are.** (Col. 3.11) The Gospel places no demands on any seeker to change their culture as a prerequisite for coming to Jesus; they may come just as they are.

5. **Avoid a fortress mentality.** (Acts 1.8) The goal of missions is not to create an impregnable castle in the midst of an unsaved community, but a dynamic outpost of the Kingdom which launches a witness for Jesus within and unto the very borders of their world.

6. **Continue to evangelize to avoid stagnation.** (Rom. 1.16-17) Keep looking to the horizons with the vision of the Great Commission in mind; foster an environment of aggressive witness for Christ.

7. **Cross racial, class, gender, and language barriers.** (1 Cor. 9.19-22) Use your freedom in Christ to find new, credible ways to communicate the kingdom message to those farthest from the cultural spectrum of the traditional church.

8. **Respect the dominance of the receiving culture.** (Acts 15.23-29) Allow the Holy Spirit to incarnate the vision and the ethics of the Kingdom of God in the words, language, customs, styles, and experience of those who have embraced Jesus as their Lord.

9. **Avoid dependence.** (Eph. 4.11-16) Neither patronize nor be overly stingy towards the growing congregation; do not underestimate the power of the Spirit in the midst of even the smallest Christian community to accomplish God's work in their community.

10. **Think reproducibility.** (2 Tim. 2.2; Phil. 1.18) In every activity and project you initiate, think in terms of equipping others to do the same by maintaining an open mind regarding the means and ends of your missionary endeavors.

APPENDIX 6

Authentic Freedom in Jesus Christ

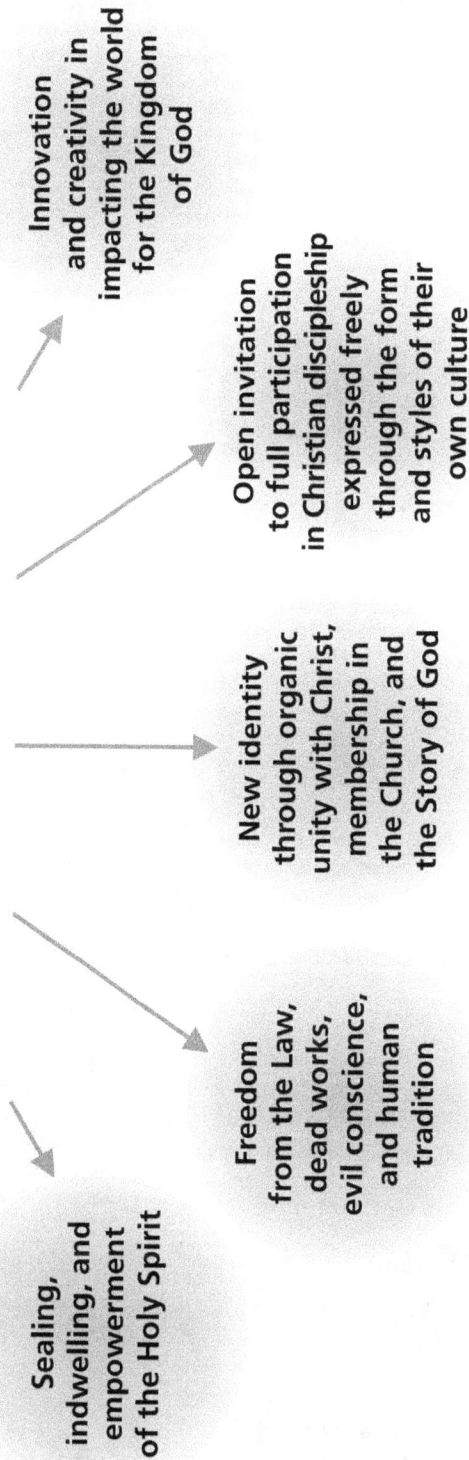

Rev. Dr. Don L. Davis

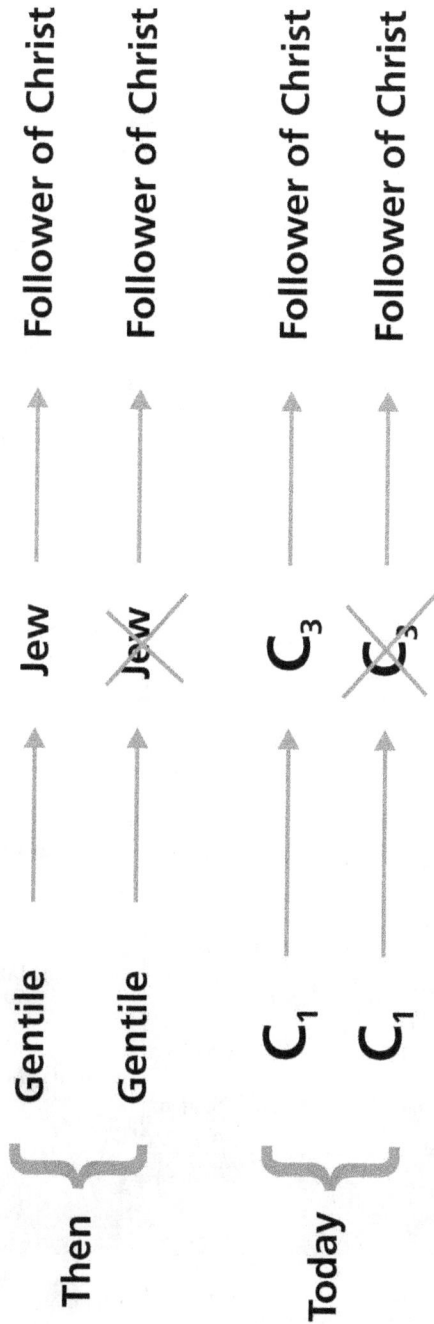

Then
{
Gentile → Follower of Christ

Jew → Follower of Christ

Gentile → Follower of Christ

~~Jew~~ → Follower of Christ
}

Today
{
C_1 → Follower of Christ

C_3 → Follower of Christ

C_1 → Follower of Christ

~~C_3~~ → Follower of Christ
}

Authentic Freedom in Jesus Christ!

Sealing, indwelling, and empowerment of the Holy Spirit

Freedom from the Law, dead works, evil conscience, and human tradition

New identity through organic unity with Christ, membership in the Church, and the Story of God

Open invitation to full participation in Christian discipleship expressed freely through the form and styles of their own culture

Innovation and creativity in impacting the world for the Kingdom of God

APPENDIX 7
The Capstone Curriculum
The Urban Ministry Institute

The Capstone Curriculum			
Developing Urban Christian Leaders for the Church and the Kingdom – Matthew 21.42			
Biblical Studies *The Lord God • Matt. 4.4*	Theology and Ethics *The Kingdom • Matt. 6.9-10*	Christian Ministry *The Church • Matt. 16.18-19*	Urban Mission *The World • Matt. 5.14-16*
1 Conversion and Calling	**2** The Kingdom of God	**3** Theology of the Church	**4** Foundations for Christian Mission
The Word That Creates The Word That Convicts The Word That Converts The Word That Calls	God's Reign Challenged God's Reign Inaugurated God's Reign Invading God's Reign Consummated	The Church Foreshadowed in God's Plan The Church at Worship The Church as Witness The Church at Work	The Vision and Biblical Foundation for Christian Mission I The Vision and Biblical Foundation for Christian Mission II Christian Mission and the City Christian Mission and the Poor
5 Bible Interpretation	**6** God the Father	**7** Foundations of Christian Leadership	**8** Evangelism and Spiritual Warfare
Biblical Inspiration: The Origins and Authority of the Bible Biblical Hermeneutics: The Three-Step Model Biblical Literature: Interpreting the Genres of the Bible Biblical Studies: Using Study Tools in Bible Study	Prolegomena: The Doctrine of God and the Advance of the Kingdom God as Creator: The Providence of God The Triune God: The Greatness of God God as Father: The Goodness of God	The Christian Leader as Deacon The Christian Leader as Elder The Christian Leader as Pastor The Christian Leader as Bishop	Spiritual Warfare: Binding of the Strong Man Evangelism: The Content of the Good News of the Kingdom Evangelism: Methods to Reach the Urban Community Follow-up and Incorporation
9 The Old Testament Witness to Christ and His Kingdom	**10** God the Son	**11** Practicing Christian Leadership	**12** Focus on Reproduction
The Promise Given The Promise Clarified The Promise Personalized The Promise Universalized	Jesus, Messiah and Lord of All: He Came Jesus, Messiah and Lord of All: He Lived Jesus, Messiah and Lord of All: He Died Jesus, Messiah and Lord of All: He Rose and Will Return	Effective Worship Leading: Worship, Word, and Sacrament Effective Christian Education: Incorporating, Parenting, and Discipling Effective Church Discipline: Exhorting, Rebuking, and Restoring Effective Counseling: Preparing, Caring, and Healing	Church Growth: Reproducing in Number and Quality Planting Urban Churches: Sowing Planting Urban Churches: Tending Planting Urban Churches: Reaping
13 The New Testament Witness to Christ and His Kingdom	**14** God the Holy Spirit	**15** The Equipping Ministry	**16** Doing Justice and Loving Mercy: Compassion Ministries
The Messiah Announced The Messiah Opposed The Messiah Revealed The Messiah Vindicated	The Person of the Holy Spirit The Prophetic Work of the Holy Spirit The Powerful Presence of the Holy Spirit I The Powerful Presence of the Holy Spirit II	The Ministry of Proclamation: Kerygma I The Ministry of Proclamation: Kerygma II The Ministry of Teaching: Didache I The Ministry of Teaching: Didache II	Let Justice Roll Down: The Vision and Theology of the Kingdom Doing Justice and Loving Mercy I: The Urban Congregation Doing Justice and Loving Mercy II: Urban Community and Neighborhood Doing Justice and Loving Mercy III: Society and World

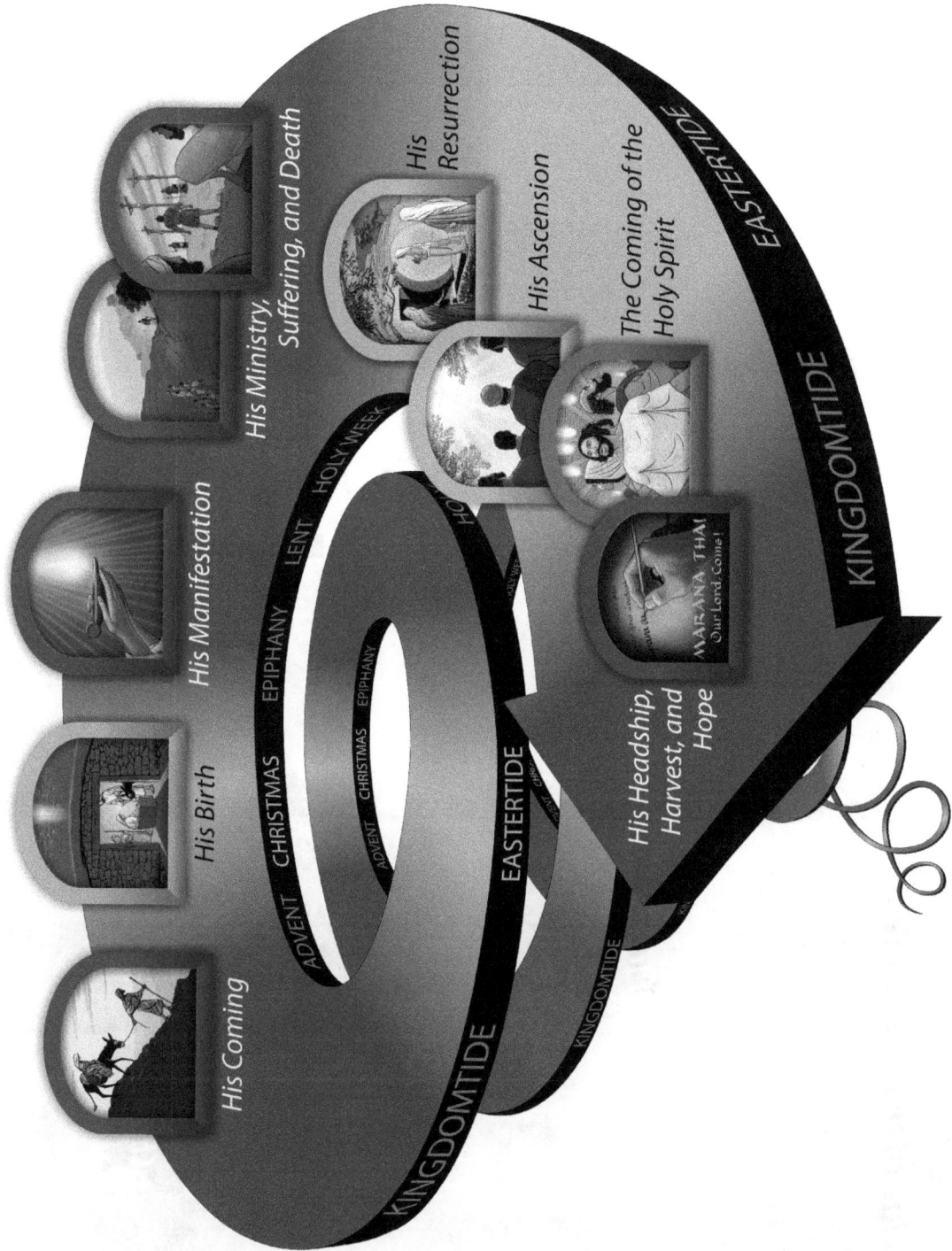

APPENDIX 8

Following the Life of Christ through Each Year

The Urban Ministry Institute

APPENDIX 9

The Plot Line of the Church Year

Rev. Ryan Carter

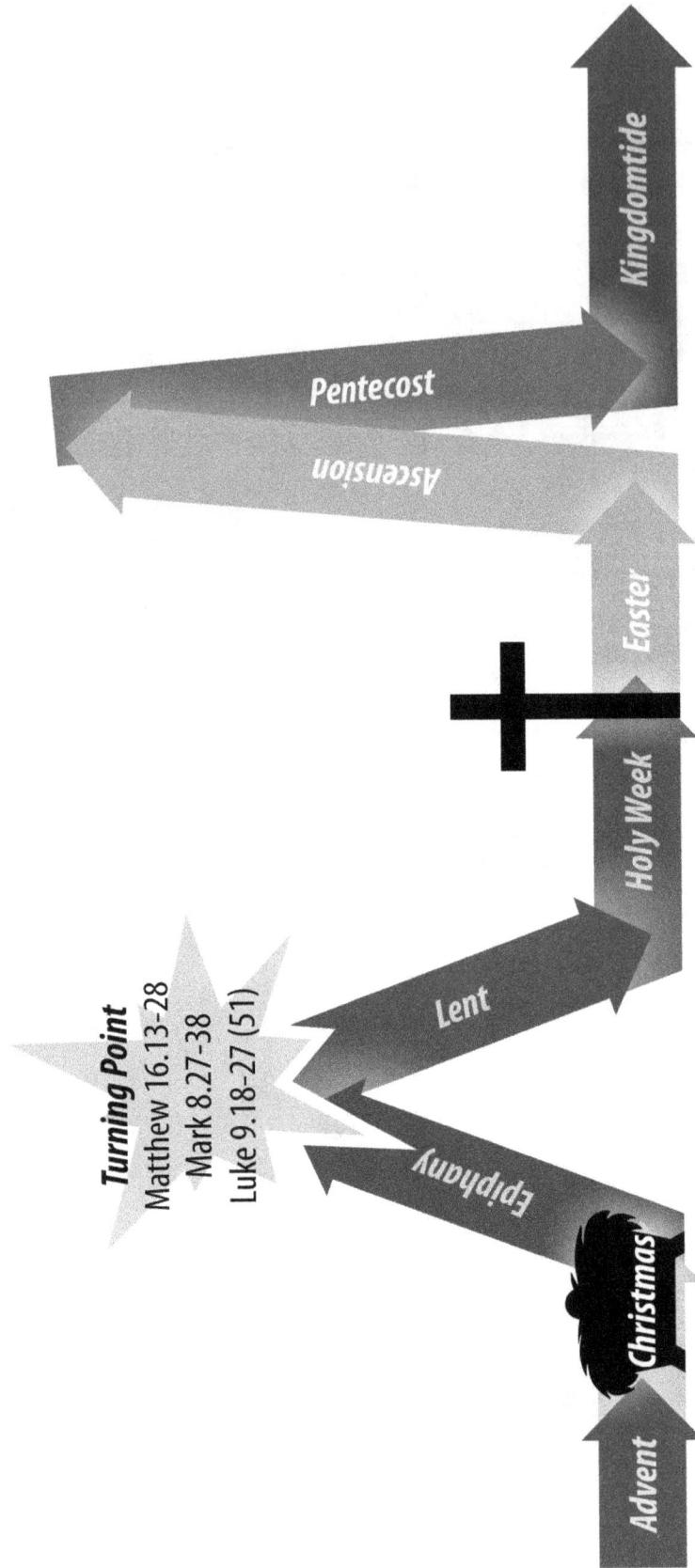

Kingdomtide

Pentecost

Ascension

Easter

Holy Week

Lent

Epiphany

Christmas

Advent

Turning Point
Matthew 16.13-28
Mark 8.27-38
Luke 9.18-27 (51)

APPENDIX 10

Christus Victor:
An Integrated Vision for the Christian Life and Witness

Rev. Dr. Don L. Davis

For the Church

- The Church is the primary extension of Jesus in the world
- Ransomed treasure of the victorious, risen Christ
- *Laos:* The people of God
- God's new creation: presence of the future
- Locus and agent of the Already/Not Yet Kingdom

For Gifts

- God's gracious endowments and benefits from *Christus Victor*
- Pastoral offices to the Church
- The Holy Spirit's sovereign dispensing of the gifts
- Stewardship: divine, diverse gifts for the common good

For Theology and Doctrine

- The authoritative Word of Christ's victory: the Apostolic Tradition: the Holy Scriptures
- Theology as commentary on the grand narrative of God
- *Christus Victor* as core theological framework for meaning in the world
- The Nicene Creed: the Story of God's triumphant grace

Christus Victor

Destroyer of Evil and Death
Restorer of Creation
Victor o'er Hades and Sin
Crusher of Satan

For Evangelism and Mission

- Evangelism as unashamed declaration and demonstration of *Christus Victor* to the world
- The Gospel as Good News of kingdom pledge
- We proclaim God's Kingdom come in the person of Jesus of Nazareth
- The Great Commission: go to all people groups making disciples of Christ and his Kingdom
- Proclaiming Christ as Lord and Messiah

For Spirituality

- The Holy Spirit's presence and power in the midst of God's people
- Sharing in the disciplines of the Spirit
- Gatherings, lectionary, liturgy, and our observances in the Church Year
- Living the life of the risen Christ in the rhythm of our ordinary lives

For Worship

- People of the Resurrection: unending celebration of the people of God
- Remembering, participating in the Christ event in our worship
- Listen and respond to the Word
- Transformed at the Table, the Lord's Supper
- The presence of the Father through the Son in the Spirit

For Justice and Compassion

- The gracious and generous expressions of Jesus through the Church
- The Church displays the very life of the Kingdom
- The Church demonstrates the very life of the Kingdom of heaven right here and now
- Having freely received, we freely give (no sense of merit or pride)
- Justice as tangible evidence of the Kingdom come

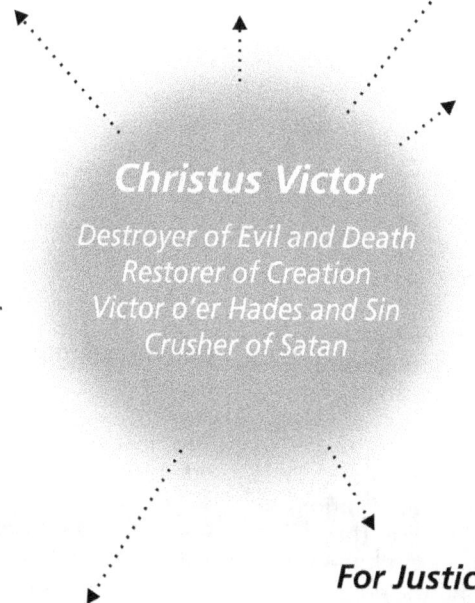

Appendix 11

Creating Coherent Urban Church Planting Movements:
Discerning the Elements of Authentic Urban Christian Community

Rev. Dr. Don L. Davis

Core Evangelical Convictions

This circle represents *its most fundamental convictions and commitments*, its Affirmation of Faith, its commitment to the Gospel and those truths contained in the early Christian creeds (i.e., The Nicene Creed). These convictions are anchored in its confidence in the Word of God, and represent our unequivocal commitment to historic orthodoxy.

As members of the one, holy, apostolic, and catholic (universal) body of Christ, movements must be **ready and willing to die for their core evangelical convictions**. These convictions serve as the connection of the movements to the historic Christian faith, and as such, can never be compromised or altered.

Distinctive Church Allegiances and Identities

This circle represents their distinctive *church allegiances and identities*. Urban church plant movements will coalesce around their own distinctive traditions, overseen by leaders who provide those movements with vision, instruction, and direction as they move forward together to represent Christ and his Kingdom in the inner city.

Specific traditions seek to express and live out this faithfulness to the Authoritative and Great Traditions through their worship, teaching, and service. They seek to make the Gospel clear within new cultures or sub-cultures, speaking and modeling the hope of Christ into new situations shaped by their own set of questions posed in light of their own unique circumstances. These movements, therefore, seek to contextualize the Authoritative Tradition in a way that faithfully and effectively leads new groups of people to faith in Jesus Christ, and incorporates those who believe into the community of faith that obeys his teachings and gives witness of him to others.

Urban church plant movements must be **ready and willing to articulate and defend their unique distinctives** as God's kingdom community in the city.

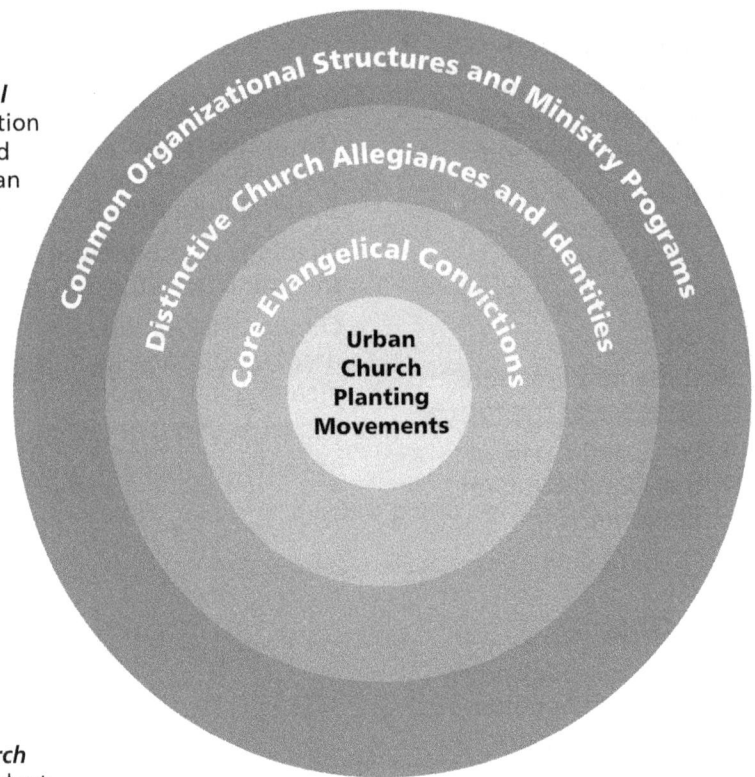

Circle diagram with concentric rings labeled from outer to inner: Common Organizational Structures and Ministry Programs, Distinctive Church Allegiances and Identities, Core Evangelical Convictions, with center labeled Urban Church Planting Movements

Common Organizational Structure and Ministry Programs

This circle represents the ways in which coherent urban church plant movements express their convictions and identity *through their own distinct organizational structures and ministry programs*. These structures and programs are designed and executed through their own specific strategies, policies, decisions, and procedures. The structures and programs represent their self-chosen methods of fleshing out their understanding of the faith as it pertains to their community purpose and mission. These are subject to change under their own legitimate processes as they apply accumulated wisdom in *how best* to accomplish their purposes in the city.

As a communities of faith in Christ, urban church movements must be encouraged to **dialogue about their structures and ministry programs** in order to discover the best possible means to contextualize the Gospel and advance the Kingdom of God among their neighbors.

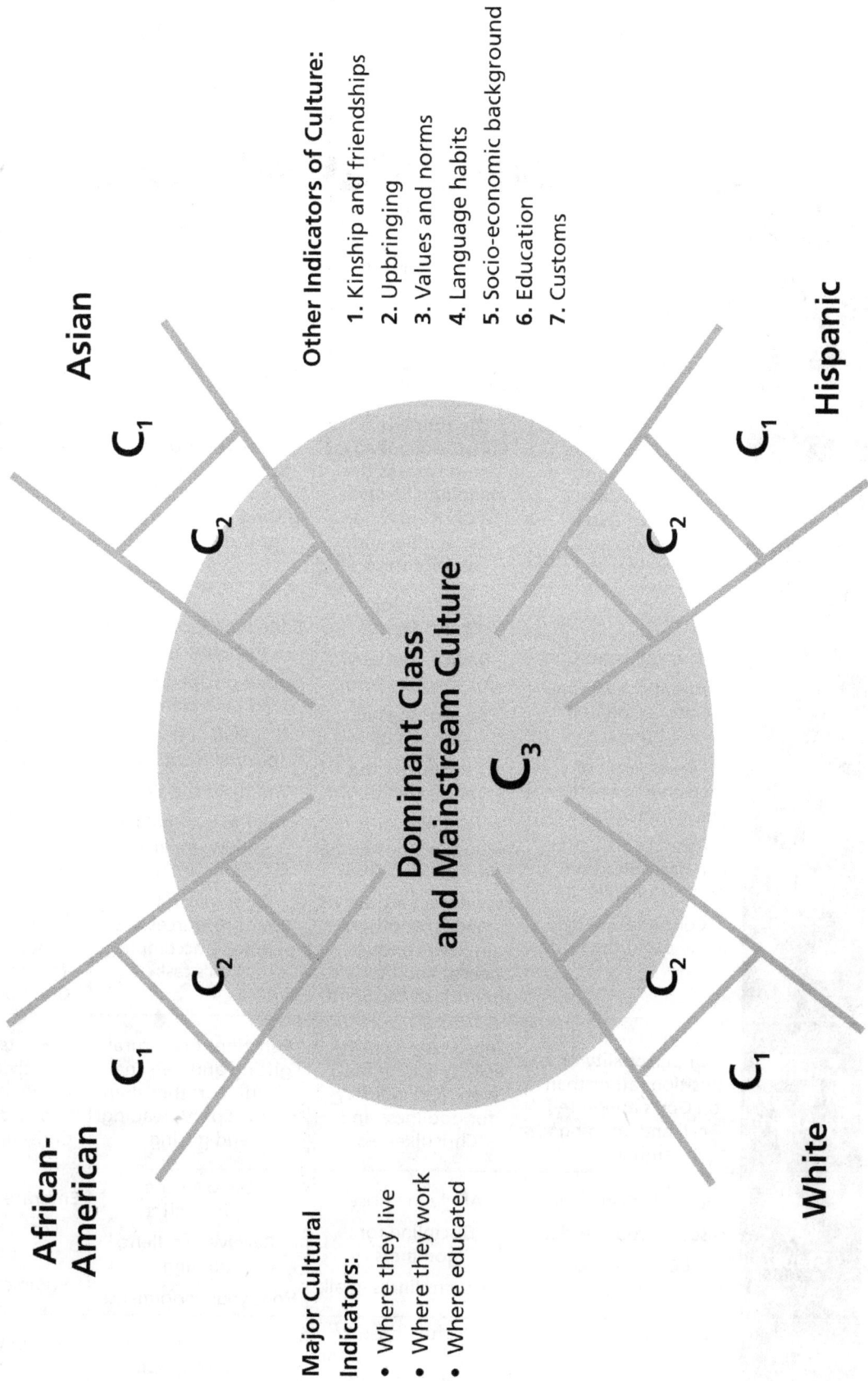

APPENDIX 12

The Interaction of Class, Culture, and Race

World Impact

Major Cultural Indicators:

- Where they live
- Where they work
- Where educated

Other Indicators of Culture:

1. Kinship and friendships
2. Upbringing
3. Values and norms
4. Language habits
5. Socio-economic background
6. Education
7. Customs

African-American

C_1

C_2

Asian

C_1

C_2

Dominant Class and Mainstream Culture

C_3

White

C_1

C_2

Hispanic

C_1

C_2

APPENDIX 13

Discipling the Faithful: Establishing Leaders for the Urban Church

Rev. Dr. Don L. Davis

	Calling	Character	Competence	Community
Definition	Recognizes *the call of God* and replies with prompt obedience to his lordship and leading	Reflects *the character of Christ* in his/her personal convictions, conduct, and lifestyle	Responds in *the power of the Spirit* with excellence in carrying out their appointed tasks and ministry	Regards multiplying disciples in *the body of Christ* as the primary role of ministry
Key Scripture	2 Tim. 1.6-14; 1 Tim. 4.14; Acts 1.8; Matt. 28.18-20	John 15.4-5; 2 Tim. 2.2; 1 Cor. 4.2; Gal. 5.16-23	2 Tim. 2.15; 3.16-17; Rom. 15.14; 1 Cor. 12	Eph. 4.9-15; 1 Cor. 12.1-27
Critical Concept	The Authority of **God**: God's leader acts on God's recognized call and authority, acknowledged by the saints and God's leaders	The Humility of **Christ**: God's leader demonstrates the mind and lifestyle of Christ in his or her actions and relationships	The Power of the **Spirit**: God's leader operates in the gifting and anointing of the Holy Spirit	The Growth of the **Church**: God's leader uses all of his or her resources to equip and empower the body of Christ for his/her goal and task
Central Elements	A clear call from God Authentic testimony before God and others Deep sense of personal conviction based on Scripture Personal burden for a particular task or people Confirmation by leaders and the body	Passion for Christlikeness Radical lifestyle for the Kingdom Serious pursuit of holiness Discipline in the personal life Fulfills role-relationships and bond-slave of Jesus Christ Provides an attractive model for others in their conduct, speech, and lifestyle (the fruit of the Spirit)	Endowments and gifts from the Spirit Sound discipling from an able mentor Skill in the spiritual disciplines Ability in the Word Able to evangelize, follow up, and disciple new converts Strategic in the use of resources and people to accomplish God's task	Genuine love for and desire to serve God's people Disciples faithful individuals Facilitates growth in small groups Pastors and equips believers in the congregation Nurtures associations and networks among Christians and churches Advances new movements among God's people locally
Satanic Strategy to Abort	Operates on the basis of personality or position rather than on God's appointed call and ongoing authority	Substitutes ministry activity and/or hard work and industry for godliness and Christlikeness	Functions on natural gifting and personal ingenuity rather than on the Spirit's leading and gifting	Exalts tasks and activities above equipping the saints and developing Christian community
Key Steps	Identify God's call Discover your burden Be confirmed by leaders	Abide in Christ Discipline for godliness Pursue holiness in all	Discover the Spirit's gifts Receive excellent training Hone your performance	Embrace God's Church Learn leadership's contexts Equip concentrically
Results	Deep confidence in God arising from God's call	Powerful Christlike example provided for others to follow	Dynamic working of the Holy Spirit	Multiplying disciples in the Church

APPENDIX 14

Fit to Represent: Multiplying Disciples of the Kingdom of God

Rev. Dr. Don L. Davis

Luke 10.16 (ESV) - The one who hears you hears me, and the one who rejects you rejects me, and the one who rejects me rejects him who sent me.

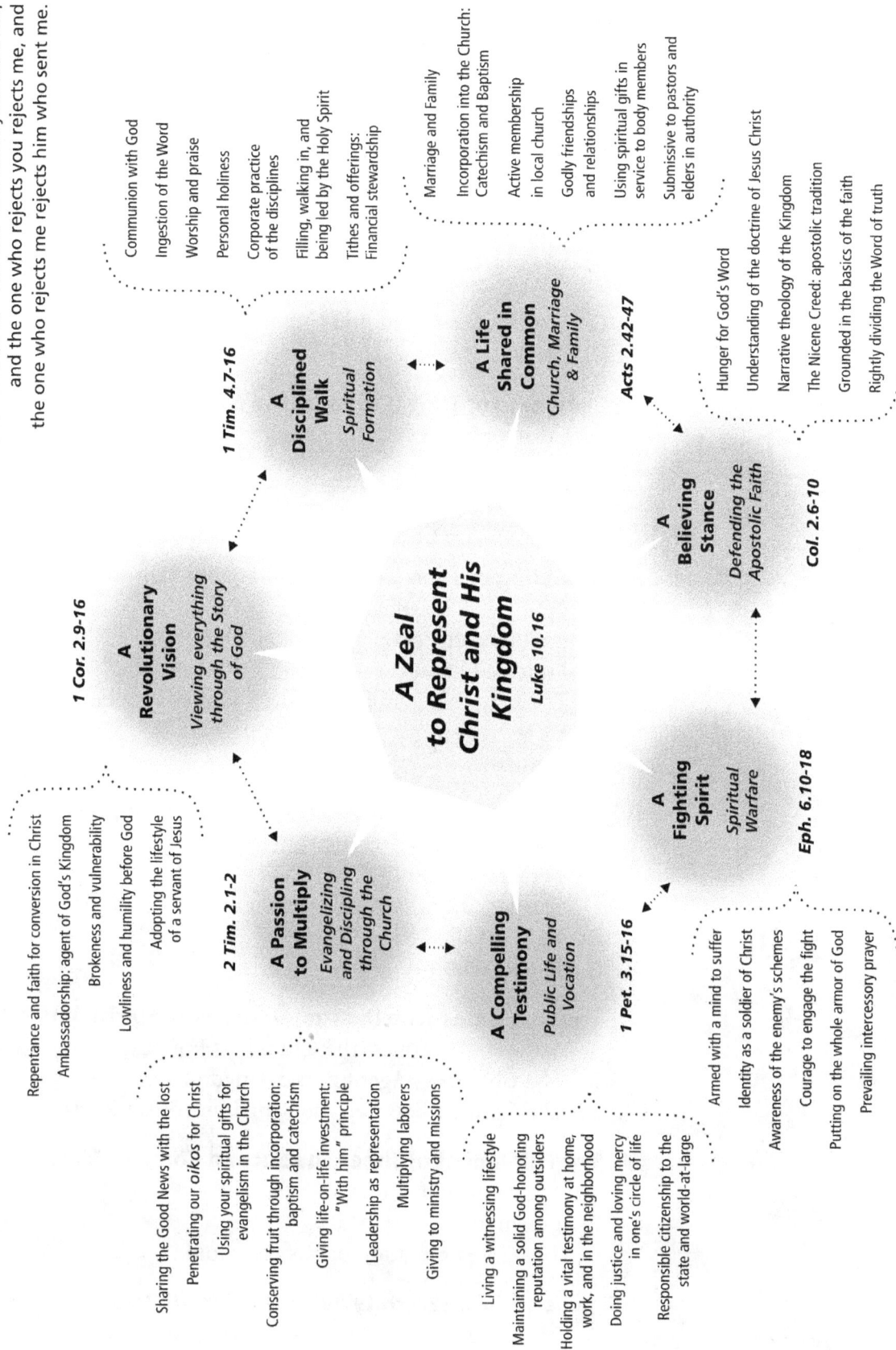

A Zeal to Represent Christ and His Kingdom
Luke 10.16

A Disciplined Walk
Spiritual Formation
1 Tim. 4.7-16

- Communion with God
- Ingestion of the Word
- Worship and praise
- Personal holiness
- Corporate practice of the disciplines
- Filling, walking in, and being led by the Holy Spirit
- Tithes and offerings: Financial stewardship

A Life Shared in Common
Church, Marriage & Family
Acts 2.42-47

- Marriage and Family
- Incorporation into the Church: Catechism and Baptism
- Active membership in local church
- Godly friendships and relationships
- Using spiritual gifts in service to body members
- Submissive to pastors and elders in authority

A Revolutionary Vision
Viewing everything through the Story of God
1 Cor. 2.9-16

A Believing Stance
Defending the Apostolic Faith
Col. 2.6-10

- Hunger for God's Word
- Understanding of the doctrine of Jesus Christ
- Narrative theology of the Kingdom
- The Nicene Creed: apostolic tradition
- Grounded in the basics of the faith
- Rightly dividing the Word of truth

A Passion to Multiply
Evangelizing and Discipling through the Church
2 Tim. 2.1-2

- Repentance and faith for conversion in Christ
- Ambassadorship: agent of God's Kingdom
- Brokenness and vulnerability
- Lowliness and humility before God
- Adopting the lifestyle of a servant of Jesus

- Sharing the Good News with the lost
- Penetrating our *oikos* for Christ
- Using your spiritual gifts for evangelism in the Church
- Conserving fruit through incorporation: baptism and catechism
- Giving life-on-life investment: "With him" principle
- Leadership as representation
- Multiplying laborers
- Giving to ministry and missions

A Compelling Testimony
Public Life and Vocation
1 Pet. 3.15-16

- Living a witnessing lifestyle
- Maintaining a solid God-honoring reputation among outsiders
- Holding a vital testimony at home, work, and in the neighborhood
- Doing justice and loving mercy in one's circle of life
- Responsible citizenship to the state and world-at-large

A Fighting Spirit
Spiritual Warfare
Eph. 6.10-18

- Armed with a mind to suffer
- Identity as a soldier of Christ
- Awareness of the enemy's schemes
- Courage to engage the fight
- Putting on the whole armor of God
- Prevailing intercessory prayer

APPENDIX 15

From Before to Beyond Time:
The Plan of God and Human History

Adapted from Suzanne de Dietrich. *God's Unfolding Purpose*. Philadelphia: Westminster Press, 1976.

I. Before Time (Eternity Past) 1 Cor. 2.7
   A. The Eternal Triune God
   B. God's Eternal Purpose
   C. The Mystery of Iniquity
   D. The Principalities and Powers

II. Beginning of Time (Creation and Fall) Gen. 1.1
   A. Creative Word
   B. Humanity
   C. Fall
   D. Reign of Death and First Signs of Grace

III. Unfolding of Time (God's Plan Revealed through Israel) Gal. 3.8
   A. Promise (Patriarchs)
   B. Exodus and Covenant at Sinai
   C. Promised Land
   D. The City, the Temple, and the Throne (Prophet, Priest, and King)
   E. Exile
   F. Remnant

IV. Fullness of Time (Incarnation of the Messiah) Gal. 4.4-5
   A. The King Comes to His Kingdom
   B. The Present Reality of His Reign
   C. The Secret of the Kingdom: the Already and the Not Yet
   D. The Crucified King
   E. The Risen Lord

V. The Last Times (The Descent of the Holy Spirit) Acts 2.16-18
   A. Between the Times: the Church as Foretaste of the Kingdom
   B. The Church as Agent of the Kingdom
   C. The Conflict Between the Kingdoms of Darkness and Light

VI. The Fulfillment of Time (The Second Coming) Matt. 13.40-43
   A. The Return of Christ
   B. Judgment
   C. The Consummation of His Kingdom

VII. Beyond Time (Eternity Future) 1 Cor. 15.24-28
   A. Kingdom Handed Over to God the Father
   B. God as All in All

From Before to Beyond Time: Scriptures for Major Outlines Points

I. Before Time (Eternity Past)
1 Cor. 2.7 (ESV) – But we impart a secret and hidden wisdom of God, which God decreed before the ages for our glory (cf. Titus 1.2).

II. Beginning of Time (Creation and Fall)
Gen. 1.1 (ESV) – In the beginning, God created the heavens and the earth.

III. Unfolding of Time (God's Plan Revealed Through Israel)
Gal. 3.8 (ESV) – And the Scripture, foreseeing that God would justify the Gentiles by faith, preached the Gospel beforehand to Abraham, saying, "In you shall all the nations be blessed" (cf. Rom. 9.4-5).

IV. Fullness of Time (The Incarnation of the Messiah)
Gal. 4.4-5 (ESV) – But when the fullness of time had come, God sent forth his Son, born of woman, born under the law, to redeem those who were under the law, so that we might receive adoption as sons.

V. The Last Times (The Descent of the Holy Spirit)
Acts 2.16-18 (ESV) – But this is what was uttered through the prophet Joel: "'And in the last days it shall be,' God declares, 'that I will pour out my Spirit on all flesh, and your sons and your daughters shall prophesy, and your young men shall see visions, and your old men shall dream dreams; even on my male servants and female servants in those days I will pour out my Spirit, and they shall prophesy.'"

VI. The Fulfillment of Time (The Second Coming)
Matt. 13.40-43 (ESV) – Just as the weeds are gathered and burned with fire, so will it be at the close of the age. The Son of Man will send his angels, and they will gather out of his Kingdom all causes of sin and all lawbreakers, and throw them into the fiery furnace. In that place there will be weeping and gnashing of teeth. Then the righteous will shine like the sun in the Kingdom of their Father. He who has ears, let him hear.

VII. Beyond Time (Eternity Future)
1 Cor. 15.24-28 (ESV) – Then comes the end, when he delivers the Kingdom to God the Father after destroying every rule and every authority and power. For he must reign until he has put all his enemies under his feet. The last enemy to be destroyed is death. For "God has put all things in subjection under his feet." But when it says, "all things are put in subjection," it is plain that he is excepted who put all things in subjection under him. When all things are subjected to him, then the Son himself will also be subjected to him who put all things in subjection under him, that God may be all in all.

APPENDIX 16

From Deep Ignorance to Credible Witness

Rev. Dr. Don L. Davis

Witness - Ability to give witness and teach
2 Tim. 2.2
Matt. 28.18-20
1 John 1.1-4
Prov. 20.6
2 Cor. 5.18-21

And the things you have heard me say in the presence of many witnesses entrust to reliable men who will also be qualified to teach others.
~ 2 Tim. 2.2

8

Lifestyle - Consistent appropriation and habitual practice based on beliefs
Heb. 5.11-6.2
Eph. 4.11-16
2 Pet. 3.18
1 Tim. 4.7-10

And Jesus increased in wisdom and in stature, and in favor with God and man.
~ Luke 2.52

7

Demonstration - Expressing conviction in corresponding conduct, speech, and behavior
James 2.14-26
2 Cor. 4.13
2 Pet. 1.5-9
1 Thess. 1.3-10

Nevertheless, at your word I will let down the net.
~ Luke 5.5

6

Conviction - Committing oneself to think, speak, and act in light of information
Heb. 2.3-4
Heb. 11.1, 6
Heb. 3.15-19
Heb. 4.2-6

Do you believe this?
~ John 11.26

5

Discernment - Understanding the meaning and implications of information
John 16.13
Eph. 1.15-18
Col. 1.9-10
Isa. 6.10; 29.10

Do you understand what you are reading?
~ Acts 8.30

4

Knowledge - Ability to recall and recite information
2 Tim. 3.16-17
1 Cor. 2.9-16
1 John 2.20-27
John 14.26

For what does the Scripture say?
~ Rom. 4.3

3

Interest - Responding to ideas or information with both curiosity and openness
Ps. 42.1-2
Acts 9.4-5
John 12.21
1 Sam. 3.4-10

We will hear you again on this matter.
~ Acts 17.32

2

Awareness - General exposure to ideas and information
Mark 7.6-8
Acts 19.1-7
John 5.39-40
Matt. 7.21-23

At that time, Herod the tetrarch heard about the fame of Jesus.
~ Matt. 14.1

1

Ignorance - Unfamiliarity with information due to naivete, indifference, or hardness
Eph. 4.17-19
Ps. 2.1-3
Rom. 1.21; 2.19
1 John 2.11

Who is the Lord that I should heed his voice?
~ Exod. 5.2

0

How to PLANT a Church

Rev. Dr. Don L. Davis

Evangelize

> Mark 16.15-18 (ESV) – And he said to them, "Go into all the world and proclaim the gospel to the whole creation. [16] Whoever believes and is baptized will be saved, but whoever does not believe will be condemned. [17] And these signs will accompany those who believe: in my name they will cast out demons; they will speak in new tongues; [18] they will pick up serpents with their hands; and if they drink any deadly poison, it will not hurt them; they will lay their hands on the sick, and they will recover."

I. Prepare

Luke 24.46-49 (ESV) – and he said to them, "Thus it is written, that the Christ should suffer and on the third day rise from the dead, and that repentance and forgiveness of sins should be proclaimed in his name to all nations, beginning from Jerusalem. You are witnesses of these things. And behold, I am sending the promise of my Father upon you. But stay in the city until you are clothed with power from on high."

A. Form a church-plant team.

B. Pray.

C. Select a target area and population.

D. Do demographic and ethnographic studies.

II. Launch

Gal. 2.7-10 (ESV) – On the contrary, when they saw that I had been entrusted with the gospel to the uncircumcised, just as Peter had been entrusted with the gospel to the circumcised (for he who worked through Peter for his apostolic ministry to the circumcised worked also through me for mine to the Gentiles), and when James and Cephas and John, who seemed to be pillars, perceived the grace that was given to me, they gave the right hand of fellowship to Barnabas and me, that we should go to the Gentiles and they to the circumcised. Only, they asked us to remember the poor, the very thing I was eager to do.

A. Recruit and train volunteers.

B. Conduct evangelistic events and door-to-door evangelism.

Equip

> Eph. 4.11-16 (ESV) – And he gave the apostles, the prophets, the evangelists, the pastors and teachers, [12] to equip the saints for the work of ministry, for building up the body of Christ, [13] until we all attain to the unity of the faith and of the knowledge of the Son of God, to mature manhood, to the measure of the stature of the fullness of Christ, [14] so that we may no longer be children, tossed to and fro by the waves and carried about by every wind of doctrine, by human cunning, by craftiness in deceitful schemes. [15] Rather, speaking the truth in love, we are to grow up in every way into him who is the head, into Christ, [16] from whom the whole body, joined and held together by every joint with which it is equipped, when each part is working properly, makes the body grow so that it builds itself up in love.

III. Assemble

Acts 2.41-47 (ESV) – So those who received his word were baptized, and there were added that day about three thousand souls. And they devoted themselves to the apostles' teaching and fellowship, to the breaking of bread and the prayers. And awe came upon every soul, and many wonders and signs were being done through the apostles. And all who believed were together and had all things in common. And they were selling their possessions and belongings and distributing the proceeds to all, as any had need. And day by day, attending the temple together and breaking bread in their homes, they received their food with glad and generous hearts, praising God and having favor with all the people. And the Lord added to their number day by day those who were being saved.

A. Form cell groups, Bible studies, etc. to follow up new believers, to continue evangelism, and to identify and train emerging leaders.

B. Announce the birth of a new church to the neighborhood and meet regularly for public worship, instruction and fellowship.

IV. Nurture

1 Thess. 2.5-9 (ESV) – For we never came with words of flattery, as you know, nor with a pretext for greed – God is witness. Nor did we seek glory from people, whether from you or from others, though we could have made demands as apostles of Christ. But we were gentle among you, like a nursing mother taking care of her own children. So, being affectionately desirous of you, we were ready to share with you not only the gospel of God but also our own selves, because you had become very dear to us. For you remember, brothers, our labor and toil: we worked night and day, that we might not be a burden to any of you, while we proclaimed to you the gospel of God.

A. Develop individual and group discipleship.

B. Fill key roles in the church: identify and use spiritual gifts.

Empower

Acts 20.28 (ESV) – Pay careful attention to yourselves and to all the flock, in which the Holy Spirit has made you overseers, to care for the church of God, which he obtained with his own blood.

Acts 20.32(ESV) – And now I commend you to God and to the word of his grace, which is able to build you up and to give you the inheritance among all those who are sanctified.

V. Transition

Titus 1.4-5 (ESV) – To Titus, my true child in a common faith: Grace and peace from God the Father and Christ Jesus our Savior. This is why I left you in Crete, so that you might put what remained into order, and appoint elders in every town as I directed you –

A. Transfer leadership to indigenous leaders so they become self-governing, self-supporting and self-reproducing (appoint elders and pastors).

B. Finalize decisions about denominational or other affiliations.

C. Commission the church.

D. Foster association with World Impact and other urban churches for fellowship, support, and mission ministry.

How to PLANT a Church

Evangelize

PREPARE
- Form a church-plant team.
- Pray.
- Select a target area and population.
- Do demographic and ethnographic studies.

LAUNCH
- Recruit and train volunteers.
- Conduct evangelistic events and door-to-door evangelism.

Equip

ASSEMBLE
- Form cell groups, Bible studies, etc. to follow up new believers, to continue evangelism, and to identify and train emerging leaders.
- Announce the birth of a new church to the neighborhood and meet regularly for public worship, instruction and fellowship.

NURTURE
- Develop individual and group discipleship.
- Fill key roles in the church; identify and use spiritual gifts.

Empower

TRANSITION
- Transfer leadership to indigenous leaders so they become self-governing, self-supporting and self-reproducing (appoint elders and pastors).
- Finalize decisions about denominational or other affiliations.
- Commission the church.
- Foster association with World Impact and other urban churches for fellowship, support and mission ministry.

Pauline Precedents from Acts: The Pauline Cycle

1. Missionaries Commissioned: Acts 13.1-4; 15.39-40; Gal. 1.15-16.
2. Audience Contacted: Acts 13.14-16; 14.1; 16.13-15; 17.16-19.
3. Gospel Communicated: Acts 13.17-41; 16.31; Rom. 10.9-14; 2 Tim. 2.8.
4. Hearers Converted: Acts. 13.48; 16.14-15; 20.21; 26.20; 1 Thess. 1.9-10.
5. Believers Congregated: Acts 13.43; 19.9; Rom 16.4-5; 1 Cor. 14.26.
6. Faith Confirmed: Acts 14.21-22; 15.41; Rom 16.17; Col. 1.28; 2 Thess. 2.15; 1 Tim. 1.3.

7. Leadership Consecrated; Acts 14.23; 2 Tim. 2.2; Titus 1.5.

8. Believers Commended; Acts 14.23; 16.40; 21.32 (2 Tim. 4.9 and Titus 3.12 by implication).

9. Relationships Continued: Acts 15.36; 18.23; 1 Cor. 16.5; Eph. 6.21-22; Col. 4.7-8.

10. Sending Churches Convened: Acts 14.26-27; 15.1-4.

The "Pauline Cycle" terminology, stages, and diagram are taken from David J. Hesselgrave, *Planting Churches Cross-Culturally,* 2nd ed. Grand Rapids: Baker Book House, 2000.

"Evangelize, Equip, and Empower" and "P.L.A.N.T." schemas for church planting taken from *Crowns of Beauty: Planting Urban Churches Conference Binder* Los Angeles: World Impact Press, 1999.

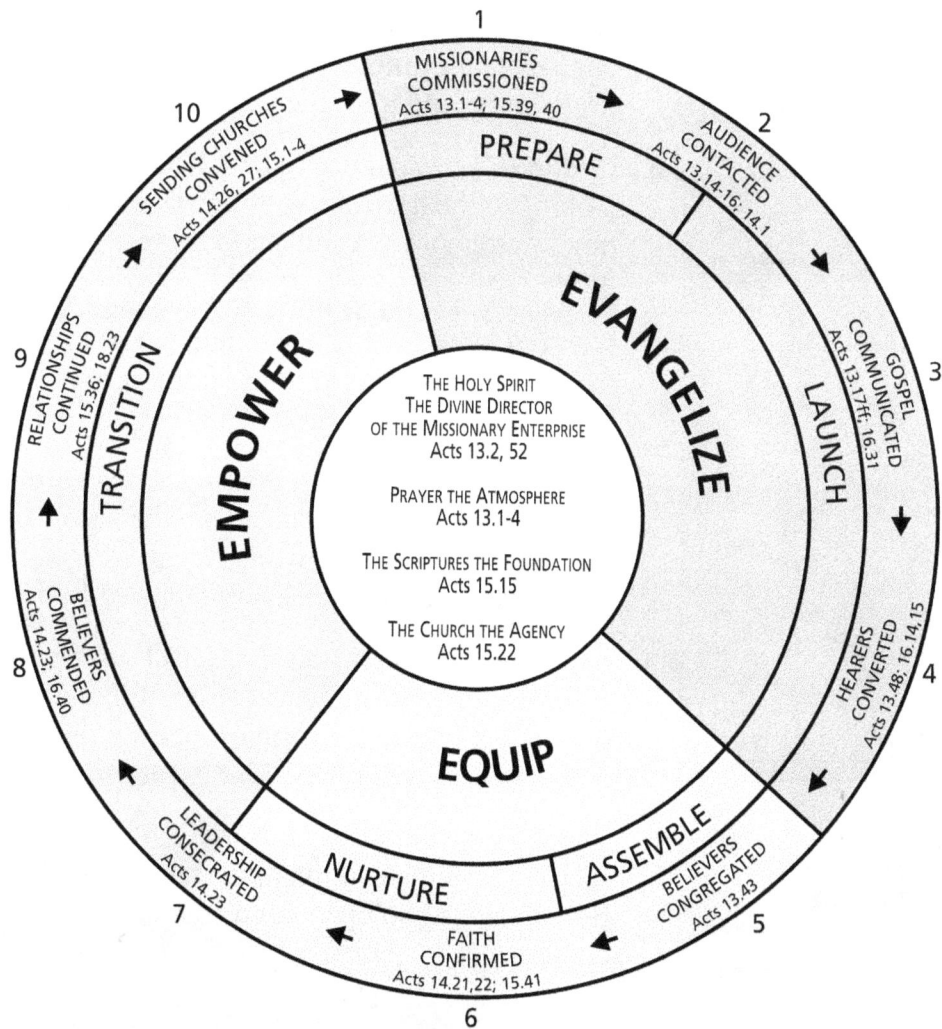

Ten Principles of Church Planting

1. **Jesus is Lord.** (Matt. 9.37-38) All church plant activity is made effective and fruitful under the watch care and power of the Lord Jesus, who himself is the Lord of the harvest.

2. **Evangelize, Equip, and Empower unreached people to reach people.** (1 Thess. 1.6-8) Our goal in reaching others for Christ is not only for solid conversion but also for dynamic multiplication; those who are reached must be trained to reach others as well.

3. **Be inclusive: whosoever will may come.** (Rom. 10.12) No strategy should forbid any person or group from entering into the Kingdom through Jesus Christ by faith.

4. **Be culturally neutral: Come just as you are.** (Col. 3.11) The Gospel places no demands on any seeker to change their culture as a prerequisite for coming to Jesus; they may come just as they are.

5. **Avoid a fortress mentality.** (Acts 1.8) The goal of missions is not to create an impregnable castle in the midst of an unsaved community, but a dynamic outpost of the Kingdom which launches a witness for Jesus within and unto the very borders of their world.

6. **Continue to evangelize to avoid stagnation.** (Rom. 1.16-17) Keep looking to the horizons with the vision of the Great Commission in mind; foster an environment of aggressive witness for Christ.

7. **Cross racial, class, gender, and language barriers.** (1 Cor. 9.19-22) Use your freedom in Christ to find new, credible ways to communicate the kingdom message to those farthest from the cultural spectrum of the traditional church.

8. **Respect the dominance of the receiving culture.** (Acts 15.23-29) Allow the Holy Spirit to incarnate the vision and the ethics of the Kingdom of God in the words, language, customs, styles, and experience of those who have embraced Jesus as their Lord.

9. **Avoid dependence.** (Eph. 4.11-16) Neither patronize nor be overly stingy towards the growing congregation; do not underestimate the power of the Spirit in the midst of even the smallest Christian community to accomplish God's work in their community.

10. **Think reproducibility.** (2 Tim. 2.2; Phil. 1.18) In every activity and project you initiate, think in terms of equipping others to do the same by maintaining an open mind regarding the means and ends of your missionary endeavors.

Resources for Further Study

Cornett, Terry G. and James D. Parker. "Developing Urban Congregations: A Framework for World Impact Church Planters." *World Impact Ministry Resources.* Los Angeles: World Impact Press, 1991.

Davis, Don L. and Terry G. Cornett. "An Outline for a Theology of the Church." *Crowns of Beauty: Planting Urban Churches* (Training Manual). Los Angeles: World Impact Press, 1999.

Hesselgrave, David J. *Planting Churches Cross Culturally: A Biblical Guide.* Grand Rapids: Baker Book House, 2000.

Hodges, Melvin L. *The Indigenous Church: A Handbook on How to Grow Young Churches.* Springfield, MO: Gospel Publishing House, 1976.

Shenk, David W. and Ervin R. Stutzman. *Creating Communities of the Kingdom: New Testament Models of Church Planting.* Scottsdale, PA: Herald Press, 1988.

APPENDIX 18

Jesus and the Poor

Rev. Dr. Don L. Davis

Thesis: The heart of Jesus's ministry of the Kingdom was the transformation and renewal of the those on the underside of life, the poor. He demonstrated his personal heart vision in how he inaugurated his ministry, authenticated his ministry, defined the heart and soul of ministry, identifying himself directly with the poor.

I. Jesus Inaugurated His Ministry with an Outreach to the Poor.

A. The inaugural sermon at Nazareth, Luke 4.16-21

Luke 4.16-21 (ESV) - And he came to Nazareth, where he had been brought up. And as was his custom, he went to the synagogue on the Sabbath day, and he stood up to read. [17] And the scroll of the prophet Isaiah was given to him. He unrolled the scroll and found the place where it was written, [18] "The Spirit of the Lord is upon me, because he has anointed me to proclaim good news to the poor. He has sent me to proclaim liberty to the captives and recovering of sight to the blind, to set at liberty those who are oppressed, [19] to proclaim the year of the Lord's favor." [20] And he rolled up the scroll and gave it back to the attendant and sat down. And the eyes of all in the synagogue were fixed on him. [21] And he began to say to them, "Today this Scripture has been fulfilled in your hearing."

B. The meaning of this inauguration

1. The object of his attention: his choice of texts

2. The object of his calling: his Spirit anointing

3. The objects of his love:

a. Good news to the poor

b. Release to the captives

c. Recovery of sight to the blind

d. Letting the oppressed go free

4. The object of his ministry: the Year of the Lord's favor

C. *Ministry to the poor as the cornerstone of his inaugural ministry*

II. Jesus Authenticated His Ministry by His Actions toward the Poor.

A. John's query regarding Jesus's authenticity, Luke 7.18-23

Luke 7.18-23 (ESV) - The disciples of John reported all these things to him. And John, [19] calling two of his disciples to him, sent them to the Lord, saying, "Are you the one who is to come, or shall we look for another?" [20] And when the men had come to him, they said, "John the Baptist has sent us to you, saying, 'Are you the one who is to come, or shall we look for another?'" [21] In that hour he healed many people of diseases and plagues and evil spirits, and on many who were blind he bestowed sight. [22] And he answered them, "Go and tell John what you have seen and heard: the BLIND RECEIVE THEIR SIGHT, the lame walk, lepers are cleansed, and the deaf hear, the dead are raised up, the POOR HAVE GOOD NEWS PREACHED TO THEM. [23] And blessed is the one who is not offended by me."

B. Will the real Messiah please stand up?

1. The question of John, 19-20

2. The actions of Jesus, 21 (the show-side of "show-and-tell")

3. The explanation of his identity, 22-23

   a. Go and tell John what you have seen and heard.

   b. Blind seeing, lame walking, lepers cleansed, deaf hearing, dead being raising, the poor hearing the Gospel

C. *Ministry to the poor is undeniable proof of the Messiah's identity.*

III. Jesus Verified Salvation in Relation to One's Treatment of the Poor.

A. The story of Zaccheus, Luke 19.1-9

Luke 19.1-9 (ESV) - He entered Jericho and was passing through. [2] And there was a man named Zacchaeus. He was a chief tax collector and was rich. [3] And he was seeking to see who Jesus was, but on account of the crowd he could not, because he was small of stature. [4] So he ran on ahead and climbed up into a sycamore tree to see him, for he was about to pass that way. [5] And when Jesus came to the place, he looked up and said to him, "Zacchaeus, hurry and come down, for I must stay at your house today." [6] So he hurried and came down and received him joyfully. [7] And when they saw it, they all grumbled, "He has gone in to be the guest of a man who is a sinner." [8] And Zacchaeus stood and said to the Lord, "Behold, Lord, the half of my goods I give to the poor. And if I have defrauded anyone of anything, I restore it fourfold." [9] And Jesus said to him, "Today salvation has come to this house, since he also is a son of Abraham."

1. The palpitations of Zaccheus

2. The salutation of Zaccheus (to Jesus)

3. The declaration of Zaccheus

   a. Half of all I own I give to the poor.

   b. I restore those wrongly treated by me four-fold.

4. The salvation of Zaccheus, vv.9-10

B. Plucking Grain on the Sabbath, Matt.12.1-8

Matt. 12.1-8 (ESV) - At that time Jesus went through the grainfields on the Sabbath. His disciples were hungry, and they began to pluck heads of grain and to eat. [2] But when the Pharisees saw it, they said to him, "Look, your disciples are doing what is not lawful to do on the Sabbath." [3] He said to them, "Have you not read what David did when he was hungry, and those who were with him: [4] how he entered the house of God and ate the bread of the Presence, which it was not lawful for him to eat nor for those who were with him, but only for the priests? [5] Or have you not read in the Law how on the Sabbath the priests in the temple profane the Sabbath and are guiltless? [6] I tell you, something greater than the temple is here. [7] And if you had known what this means, 'I DESIRE MERCY, AND NOT SACRIFICE,' you would not have condemned the guiltless. [8] For the Son of Man is lord of the Sabbath."

1. Disciples snacking on corn on the Sabbath

2. The Pharisees disputation: "Look, your disciples are doing what is not lawful to do on the sabbath."

3. Jesus's retort: "I desire mercy and not sacrifice."

   a. Mercy to the poor and broken, not ritual faithfulness

   b. Compassion for the broken, not religious discipline

C. *Ministry to the poor is the litmus test of authentic salvation.*

IV. Jesus Identifies Himself Unreservedly with the Poor.

A. Those who cannot repay you, Luke 14.11-15

Luke 14.11-14 (ESV) - "For everyone who exalts himself will be humbled, and he who humbles himself will be exalted." [12] He said also to the man who had invited him, "When you give a dinner or a banquet, do not invite your friends or your brothers or your relatives or rich neighbors, lest they also invite you in return and you be repaid. [13] But when you give a feast, invite the poor, the crippled, the lame, the blind, [14] and you will be blessed, because they cannot repay you. You will be repaid at the resurrection of the just."

B. The Judgment Seat of the King, Matt. 25.31-45

Matt. 25.34-40 (ESV) - Then the King will say to those on his right, "Come, you who are blessed by my Father, inherit the kingdom prepared for you from the foundation of the world. [35] For I was hungry and you gave me food, I was thirsty and you gave me drink, I was a stranger and you welcomed me, [36] I was naked and you clothed me, I was sick and you visited me, I was in prison and you came to me." [37] Then the righteous will answer him, saying, "Lord, when did we see you hungry and feed you, or thirsty and give you drink? [38] And when did we see you a stranger and welcome you, or naked and clothe you? [39] And when did we see you sick or in prison and visit you?" [40] And the King will answer them, "Truly, I say to you, as you did it to one of the least of these my brothers, you did it to me."

1. Two sets of people: sheep and goats

2. Two responses: one blessed and embraced, one judged and rejected

3. Two destinies: the sheep in the Kingdom inherited, prepared from the foundation of the world, the goats in the eternal fire prepared for the devil and his angels

4. Two reactions: one was hospitable, charitable, generous; the other apathetic, heartless, negligent

5. The same group of people: the hungry, the thirsty, the stranger, the naked, the sick, the prisoner

6. *The same standard: in the way you treated or mistreated these people, those on the underside of life, so you responded to me.*

C. Jesus made it appear as those who were least deserving but repentant would become heirs of the Kingdom.

Matt. 21.31 (ESV) - "Which of the two did the will of his father?" They said, "The first." Jesus said to them, "Truly, I say to you, the tax collectors and the prostitutes go into the kingdom of God before you."

Mark 2.15-17 (ESV) - And as he reclined at table in his house, many tax collectors and sinners were reclining with Jesus and his disciples, for there were many who followed him. [16] And the scribes of the Pharisees, when they saw that he was eating with sinners and tax collectors, said to his disciples, "Why does he eat with tax collectors and sinners?" [17] And when Jesus heard it, he said to them, "Those who are well have no need of a physician, but those who are sick. I came not to call the righteous, but sinners."

D. Ministry to the poor is ministry to the Lord Jesus - his identification with them is complete.

Conclusion: The heart and soul of Jesus's ministry was directed toward the transformation and liberation of those who were most vulnerable, most forgotten, most neglected. As disciples, may we demonstrate the same.

APPENDIX 19

Leader-Follower Representation

Rev. Dr. Don L. Davis

What the Leader Provides

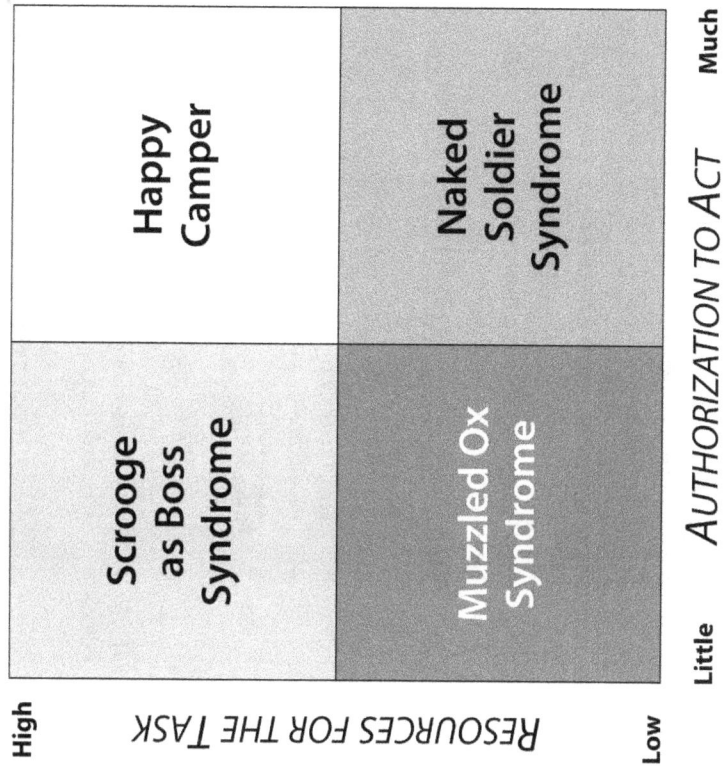

Scrooge as Boss Syndrome	**Happy Camper**
Muzzled Ox Syndrome	**Naked Soldier Syndrome**

RESOURCES FOR THE TASK — High / Low

AUTHORIZATION TO ACT — Little / Much

What the Follower Expresses

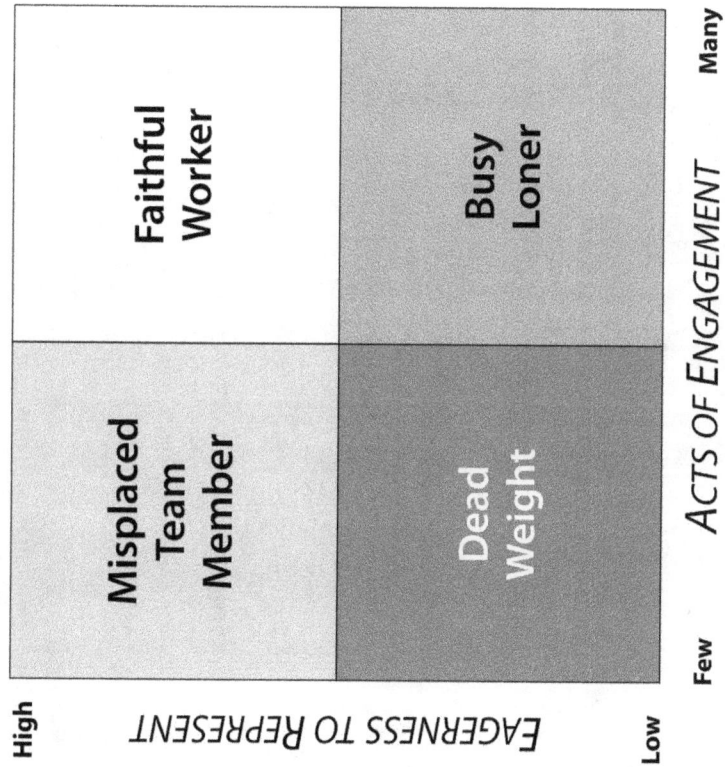

Misplaced Team Member	**Faithful Worker**
Dead Weight	**Busy Loner**

EAGERNESS TO REPRESENT — High / Low

ACTS OF ENGAGEMENT — Few / Many

APPENDIX 20

Understanding Leadership as Representation: The Six Stages of Formal Proxy

Rev. Dr. Don L. Davis

Luke 10.1 (ESV) – After this the Lord appointed seventy-two others and sent them on ahead of him, two by two, into every town and place where he himself was about to go . . . .

Luke 10.16 (ESV) – "The one who hears you hears me, and the one who rejects you rejects me, and the one who rejects me rejects him who sent me."

John 20.21 (ESV) – Jesus said to them again, "Peace be with you. As the Father has sent me, even so I am sending you."

Commissioning [1]
Formal Selection and Call to Represent
- Chosen to be an emissary, envoy, or proxy
- Confirmed by appropriate other who recognize the call
- Is recognized to be a member of a faithful community
- Calling out of a group to a particular role of representation
- Calling to a particular task or mission
- Delegation of position or responsibility

Equipping [2]
Appropriate Resourcing and Training to Fulfill the Call
- Assignment to a supervisor, superior, mentor, or instructor
- Disciplined instruction of principles underlying the call
- Constant drill, practice, and exposure to appropriate skills
- Recognition of gifts and strengths
- Expert coaching and ongoing feedback

Entrustment [3]
Corresponding Authorization and Empowerment to Act
- Delegation of authority to act and speak on commissioner's behalf
- Scope and limits of representative power provided
- Formal deputization (right to enforce and represent)
- Permission given to be an emissary (to stand in stead of)
- Release to fulfill the commission and task received

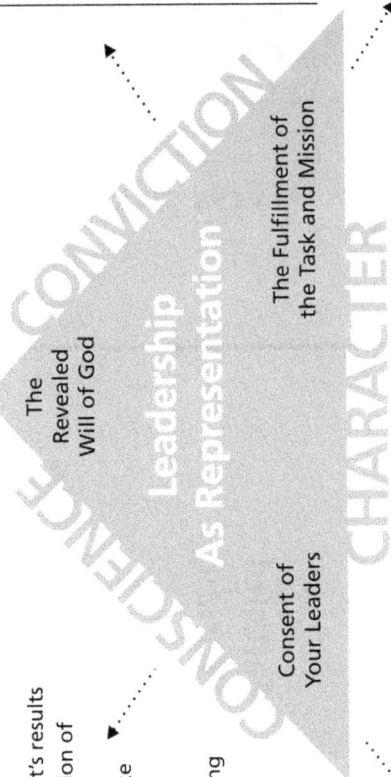

Leadership As Representation

The Revealed Will of God

The Fulfillment of the Task and Mission

Consent of Your Leaders

CONVICTION

CONSCIENCE

CHARACTER

Mission [4]
Faithful and Disciplined Engagement of the Task
- Subordination of one's will to accomplish the assignment
- Obedience: carrying out the orders of those who sent you
- Fulfilling the task that was given to you
- Freely acting within one's delegated authority to fulfill the task
- Maintaining loyalty to those who sent you
- Using all means available to do one's duty, whatever the cost
- Full recognition of one's answerability to the one(s) who commissioned

Reckoning [5]
Official Evaluation and Review of One's Execution
- Reporting back to sending authority for critical review
- Formal comprehensive assessment of one's execution and results
- Judgment of one's loyalties and faithfulness
- Sensitive analysis of what we accomplished
- Readiness to ensure that our activities and efforts produce results

Reward [6]
Public Recognition and Continuing Response
- Formal publishing of assessment's results
- Acknowledgment and recognition of behavior and conduct
- Corresponding reward or rebuke for execution
- Review made basis for possible reassignment or recommissioning
- Assigning new projects with greater authority

APPENDIX 21

Living in the Already and the Not Yet Kingdom

Rev. Dr. Don L. Davis

The Spirit: The pledge of the inheritance (*arrabon*)
The Church: The foretaste (*aparche*) of the Kingdom
"In Christ": The rich life (*en Christos*) we share as citizens of the Kingdom

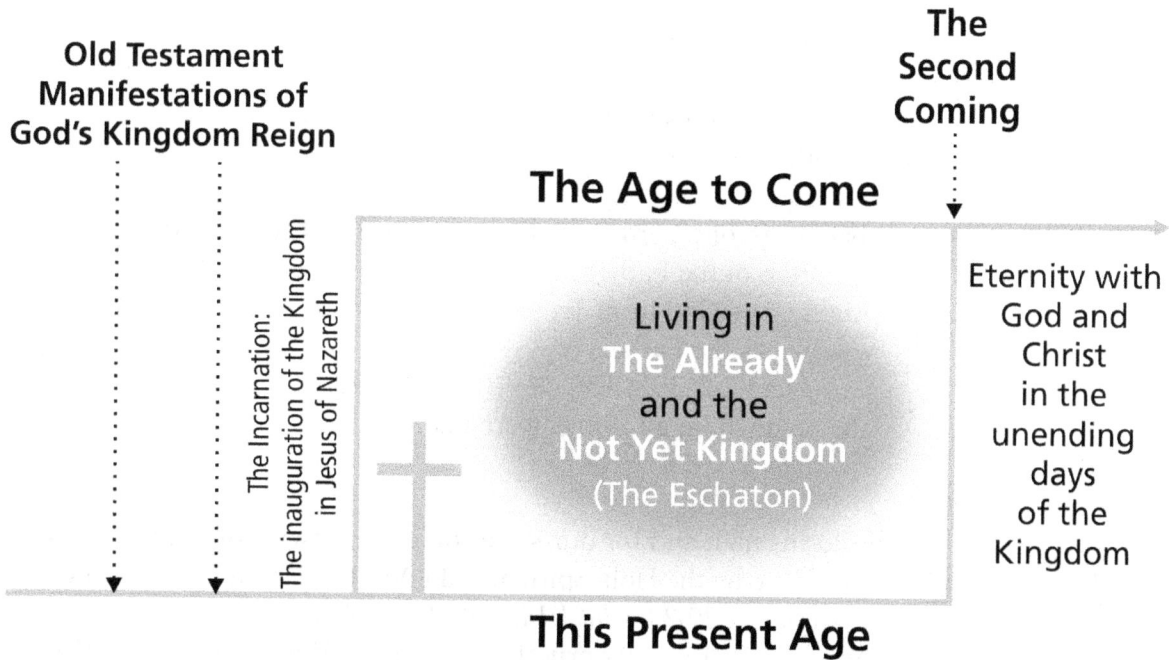

Old Testament Manifestations of God's Kingdom Reign

The Second Coming

The Age to Come

The Incarnation: The inauguration of the Kingdom in Jesus of Nazareth

Living in
The Already
and the
Not Yet Kingdom
(The Eschaton)

Eternity with God and Christ in the unending days of the Kingdom

This Present Age

Internal enemy: The flesh (*sarx*) and the sin nature
External enemy: The world (*kosmos*) the systems of greed, lust, and pride
Infernal enemy: The devil (*kakos*) the animating spirit of falsehood and fear

Jewish View of Time

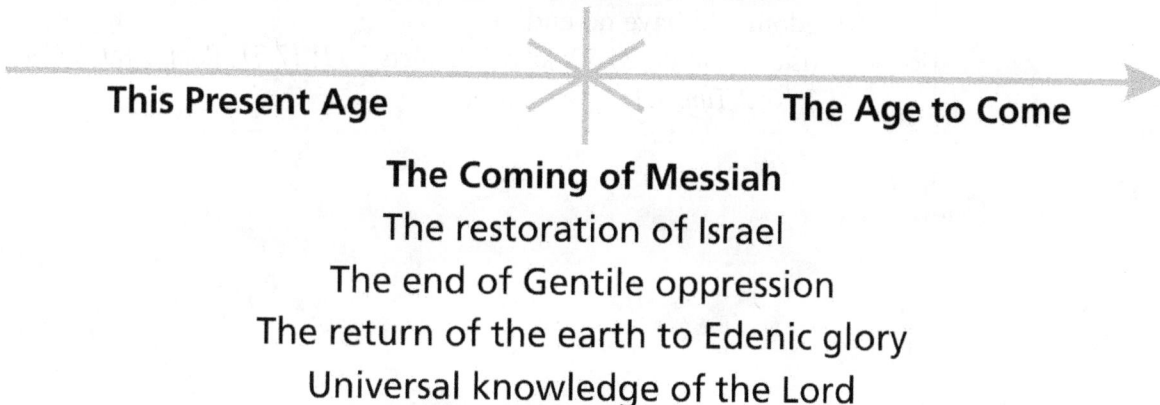

This Present Age   **The Age to Come**

The Coming of Messiah
The restoration of Israel
The end of Gentile oppression
The return of the earth to Edenic glory
Universal knowledge of the Lord

APPENDIX 22

The Nicene Creed with Biblical Support

The Urban Ministry Institute

We believe in one God,
>   (Deut. 6.4-5; Mark 12.29; 1 Cor. 8.6)
>   the Father Almighty,
>   (Gen. 17.1; Dan. 4.35; Matt. 6.9; Eph. 4.6; Rev. 1.8)
>   Maker of heaven and earth
>   (Gen. 1.1; Isa. 40.28; Rev. 10.6)
>   and of all things visible and invisible.
>   (Ps. 148; Rom. 11.36; Rev. 4.11)

We believe in one Lord Jesus Christ, the only Begotten Son of God,
begotten of the Father before all ages, God from God, Light from
Light, True God from True God, begotten not created, of the same
essence as the Father,
>   (John 1.1-2; 3.18; 8.58; 14.9-10; 20.28; Col. 1.15, 17; Heb. 1.3-6)
>   through whom all things were made.
>   (John 1.3; Col. 1.16)

Who for us men and for our salvation came down from heaven and was
incarnate by the Holy Spirit and the Virgin Mary and became human.
>   (Matt. 1.20-23; John 1.14; 6.38; Luke 19.10)
>   Who for us too, was crucified under Pontius Pilate, suffered and
>   was buried.
>   (Matt. 27.1-2; Mark 15.24-39, 43-47; Acts 13.29; Rom. 5.8; Heb. 2.10;
>   13.12)
>   The third day he rose again according to the Scriptures,
>   (Mark 16.5-7; Luke 24.6-8; Acts 1.3; Rom. 6.9; 10.9; 2 Tim. 2.8)
>   ascended into heaven, and is seated at the right hand of the Father.
>   (Mark 16.19; Eph. 1.19-20)
>   He will come again in glory to judge the living and the dead, and his
>   Kingdom will have no end.
>   (Isa. 9.7; Matt. 24.30; John 5.22; Acts 1.11; 17.31; Rom. 14.9; 2 Cor.
>   5.10; 2 Tim. 4.1)

We believe in the Holy Spirit, the Lord and life-giver,
> *(Gen. 1.1-2; Job 33.4; Ps. 104.30; 139.7-8; Luke 4.18-19;*
> *John 3.5-6; Acts 1.1-2; 1 Cor. 2.11; Rev. 3.22)*

who proceeds from the Father and the Son,
> *(John 14.16-18, 26; 15.26; 20.22)*

who together with the Father and Son is worshiped and glorified,
> *(Isa. 6.3; Matt. 28.19; 2 Cor. 13.14; Rev. 4.8)*

who spoke by the prophets.
> *(Num. 11.29; Mic. 3.8; Acts 2.17-18; 2 Pet. 1.21)*

We believe in one holy, catholic, and apostolic Church.
> *(Matt. 16.18; Eph. 5.25-28; 1 Cor. 1.2; 10.17; 1 Tim. 3.15; Rev. 7.9)*

We acknowledge one baptism for the forgiveness of sin,
> *(Acts 22.16; 1 Pet. 3.21; Eph. 4.4-5)*

And we look for the resurrection of the dead and the life of the age to come.
> *(Isa. 11.6-10; Mic. 4.1-7; Luke 18.29-30; Rev. 21.1-5; 21.22-22.5)*

Amen.

The Nicene Creed with Biblical Support – Memory Verses

Below are suggested memory verses, one for each section of the Creed.

The Father
Rev. 4.11 – Worthy are you, our Lord and God, to receive glory and honor and power, for you created all things, and by your will they existed and were created.

The Son
John 1.1 – In the beginning was the Word, and the Word was with God, and the Word was God.

The Son's Mission
1 Cor. 15.3-5 – For what I received I passed on to you as of first importance: that Christ died for our sins according to the Scriptures, that he was buried, that he was raised on the third day according to the Scriptures, and that he appeared to Peter, and then to the Twelve.

The Holy Spirit
Rom. 8.11 – If the Spirit of him who raised Jesus from the dead dwells in you, he who raised Christ Jesus from the dead will also give life to your mortal bodies through his Spirit who dwells in you.

The Church

1 Pet. 2.9 – But you are a chosen race, a royal priesthood, a holy nation, a people for his own possession, that you may proclaim the excellencies of him who called you out of darkness into his marvelous light.

Our Hope

1 Thess. 4.16-17 – For the Lord himself will descend from heaven with a cry of command, with the voice of an archangel, and with the sound of the trumpet of God. And the dead in Christ will rise first. Then we who are alive, who are left, will be caught up together with them in the clouds to meet the Lord in the air, and so we will always be with the Lord.

Once Upon a Time:
The Cosmic Drama through a Biblical Narration of the World

Rev. Dr. Don L. Davis

From everlasting to everlasting, our Lord is God

From everlasting, in that matchless mystery of existence before time began, our Triune God dwelt in perfect splendor in eternal community as Father, Son, and Holy Spirit, the I AM, displaying his perfect attributes in eternal relationship, needing nothing, in boundless holiness, joy, and beauty. According to his sovereign will, our God purposed out of love to create a universe where his splendor would be revealed, and a world where his glory would be displayed and where a people made in his own image would dwell, sharing in fellowship with him and enjoying union with himself in relationship, all for his glory.

Who, as the Sovereign God, created a world that would ultimately rebel against his rule

Inflamed by lust, greed, and pride, the first human pair rebelled against his will, deceived by the great prince, Satan, whose diabolical plot to supplant God as ruler of all resulted in countless angelic beings resisting God's divine will in the heavenlies. Through Adam and Eve's disobedience, they exposed themselves and their heirs to misery and death, and through their rebellion ushered creation into chaos, suffering, and evil. Through sin and rebellion, the union between God and creation was lost, and now all things are subject to the effects of this great fall–alienation, separation, and condemnation become the underlying reality for all things. No angel, human being, or creature can solve this dilemma, and without God's direct intervention, all the universe, the world, and all its creatures would be lost.

Yet, in mercy and loving-kindness, the Lord God promised to send a Savior to redeem his creation

In sovereign covenantal love, God determined to remedy the effects of the universe's rebellion by sending a Champion, his only Son, who would take on the form of the fallen pair, embrace and overthrow their separation from God, and suffer in the place of all humankind for its sin and disobedience. So, through his covenant faithfulness, God became directly involved in human history for the sake of their salvation. The Lord God stoops to engage his creation for the sake of restoring it, to put down evil once and for all, and to establish a people out of which his Champion would come to establish his reign in this world once more.

So, he raised up a people from which the Governor would come

And so, through Noah, he saves the world from its own evil, through Abraham, he selects the clan through which the seed would come. Through Isaac, he continues the promise to Abraham, and through Jacob (Israel) he establishes his nation, identifying the tribe out of which he will come (Judah). Through Moses, he delivers his own from oppression and gives them his covenantal law, and through Joshua, he brings his people into the land of promise. Through judges and leaders he superintends his people, and through David, he covenants to bring a King from his clan who will reign forever. Despite his promise, though, his people fall short of his covenant time after time. Their stubborn and persistent rejection of the Lord finally leads to the nation's judgment, invasion, overthrow, and captivity. Mercifully, he remembers his covenant and allows a remnant to return – for the promise and the story were not done.

**Who, as Champion, came down from heaven,
in the fullness of time, and won through the Cross**

Some four hundred years of silence occurred. Yet, in the fullness of time, God fulfilled his covenant promise by entering into this realm of evil, suffering, and alienation through the incarnation. In the person of Jesus of Nazareth, God came down from heaven and lived among us, displaying the Father's glory, fulfilling the requirements of God's moral law, and demonstrating the power of the Kingdom of God in his words, works, and exorcisms. On the Cross he took on our rebellion, destroyed death, overcame the devil, and rose on the third day to restore creation from the Fall, to make an end of sin, disease, and war, and to grant never-ending life to all people who embrace his salvation.

**And, soon and very soon,
he will return to this world and make all things new**

Ascended to the Father's right hand, the Lord Jesus Christ has sent the Holy Spirit into the world, forming a new people made up of both Jew and Gentile, the Church. Commissioned under his headship, they testify in word and deed the gospel of reconciliation to the whole creation, and when they have completed their task, he will return in glory and complete his work for creation and all creatures. Soon, he will put down sin, evil, death, and the effects of the Curse forever, and restore all creation under its true rule, refreshing all things in a new heavens and new earth, where all beings and all creation will enjoy the shalom of the triune God forever, to his glory and honor alone.

And the redeemed shall live happily ever after . . .

The End

Paul's Team Members:
Companions, Laborers, and Fellow Workers

Rev. Dr. Don L. Davis

Achaicus, a Corinthian who visited Paul at Philippi, 1 Cor. 16.17.

Archippus, Colossian disciple whom Paul exhorted to fulfill his ministry, Col. 4.17; Philem. 2.

Aquila, Jewish disciple Paul found at Corinth, Acts 18.2, 18, 26; Rom. 16.3; 1 Cor. 16.19; 2 Tim. 4.19.

Aristarchus, with Paul on 3rd journey, Acts 19.29; 20.4; 27.2; Col. 4.10; Philem. 24.

Artemas, companion of Paul at Nicopolis, Titus 3.12.

Barnabas, a Levite, cousin of John Mark, and companion with Paul in several of his journeys, cf. Acts 4.36, 9.27; 11.22, 25, 30; 12.25; chs. 13, 14, and 15; 1 Cor. 9.6; Gal. 2.1, 9, 13; Col. 4.13.

Carpus, disciple of Troas, 2 Tim. 4.13.

Claudia, female disciple of Rome, 2 Tim. 4.21.

Clement, fellow-laborer at Phillipi, Phil. 4.3.

Crescens, a disciple at Rome, 2 Tim. 4.10.

Demas, a laborer of Paul at Rome, Col. 4.14; Philem. 24; 2 Tim. 4.10.

Epaphras, fellow laborer and prisoner, Col. 1.7, 4.12; Philem. 23.

Epaphroditus, messenger between Paul and the churches, Phil. 2.25, 4.18.

Eubulus, disciple of Rome, 2 Tim. 4.21.

Euodia, Christian woman of Philippi, Phil. 4.2

Fortunatus, part of the Corinthian team, 1 Cor. 16.17.

Gaius, 1) a Macedonian companion, Acts 19.29; 2) a disciple/companion in Derbe, Acts 20.4.

Jesus (Justus), a Jewish disciple at Colossae, Col. 4.11.

John Mark, companion of Paul and cousin of Barnabas, Acts 12.12, 15; 15.37, 39; Col. 4.10; 2 Tim. 4.11; Philem. 24.

Linus, a Roman Companion of Paul, 2 Tim. 4.21.

Luke, physician and fellow-traveler with Paul, Col. 4.14; 2 Tim. 4.11; Philem. 24.

Onesimus, native of Colossae and slave of Philemon who served Paul, Col. 4.9; Philem. 10.

Hermogenes, a team member who abandoned Paul in prison, 2 Tim. 1.15.

Phygellus, one with Hermogenes turned from Paul in Asia, 2 Tim. 1.15.

Priscilla (Prisca), wife of Aquila of Pontus and fellow-worker in the Gospel, Acts 18.2, 18, 26; Rom. 16.3; 1 Cor. 16.19.

Pudens, a Roman companion of Paul, 2 Tim. 4.21.

Secundus, companion of Paul on his way from Greece to Syria, Acts 20.4.

Silas, disciple, fellow laborer, and prisoner with Paul, Acts 15.22, 27, 32, 34, 40; 16.19, 25, 29; 17.4, 10, etc.

Sopater, accompanied Paul to Syria, Acts 20.4.

Sosipater, kinsman of Paul, Rom. 16.21.

Silvanus, probably same as Silas, 2 Cor. 1.19; 1 Thess. 1.1; 2 Thess. 1.1.

Sosthenes, Chief Ruler of the Synagogue of Corinth, laborer with Paul there, Acts 18.17.

Stephanus, one of the first believers of Achaia and visitor to Paul, 1 Cor. 1.16; 16.15; 16.17.

Syntyche, one of Paul's female "fellow workers" in Philippi, Phil. 4.2.

Tertius, slave and person who wrote the Epistle to the Romans, Rom. 16.22.

Timothy, a young man of Lystra with a Jewish mother and Greek father who labored on with Paul in his ministry, Acts 16.1;17.14, 15; 18.5; 19.22; 20.4; Rom. 16.21; 1 Cor. 4.17; 16.10; 2 Cor. 1.1, 19; Phil. 1.1; 2.19; Col. 1.1; 1 Thess. 1.1; 3.2, 6; 2 Thess. 1.1; 1 Tim. 1.2, 18; 6.20; 2 Tim. 1.2; Philem. 1; Heb. 13.23.

Titus, Greek disciple and co-laborer of Paul, 2 Cor. 2.13; 7.6, 13, 14; 8.6, 16, 23; 12.18; Gal. 2.1, 3; 2 Tim. 4.10; Titus 1.4.

Trophimus, Ephesian disciple who accompanied Paul to Jerusalem from Greece, Acts 20.4; 21.29; 2 Tim. 4.20.

Tryphena and *Tryphosa*, female disciples of Rome, probably twins, who Paul calls laborers in the Lord, Rom. 16.12.

Tychicus, a disciple of Asia Minor who accompanied Paul in various trips, Acts 20.4; Eph. 6.21; Col. 4.7; 2 Tim. 4.12; Titus 3.12.

Urbanus, Roman disciple and aid to Paul, Rom. 16.9.

APPENDIX 25
A Sociology of Urban Leadership Development:
A Tool for Assessment and Training

Rev. Dr. Don L. Davis

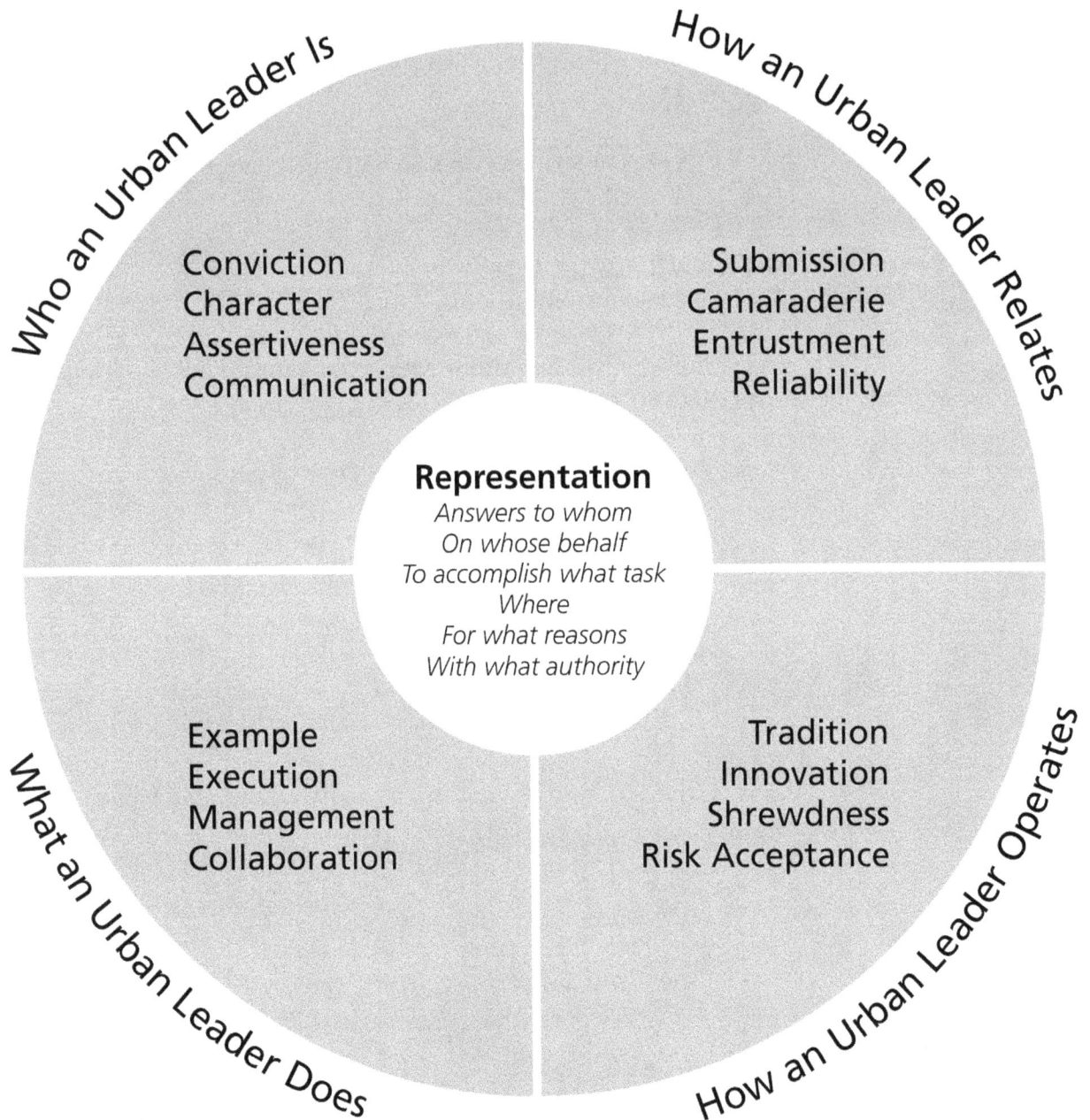

Who an Urban Leader Is

Conviction
Character
Assertiveness
Communication

How an Urban Leader Relates

Submission
Camaraderie
Entrustment
Reliability

Representation
Answers to whom
On whose behalf
To accomplish what task
Where
For what reasons
With what authority

What an Urban Leader Does

Example
Execution
Management
Collaboration

How an Urban Leader Operates

Tradition
Innovation
Shrewdness
Risk Acceptance

APPENDIX 26

Representin': Jesus as God's Chosen Representative

Rev. Dr. Don L. Davis

To represent another
Is to be selected to stand in the place of another, and thereby fulfill the assigned duties, exercise the rights and serve as deputy for, as well as to speak and act with another's authority on behalf of their interests and reputation.

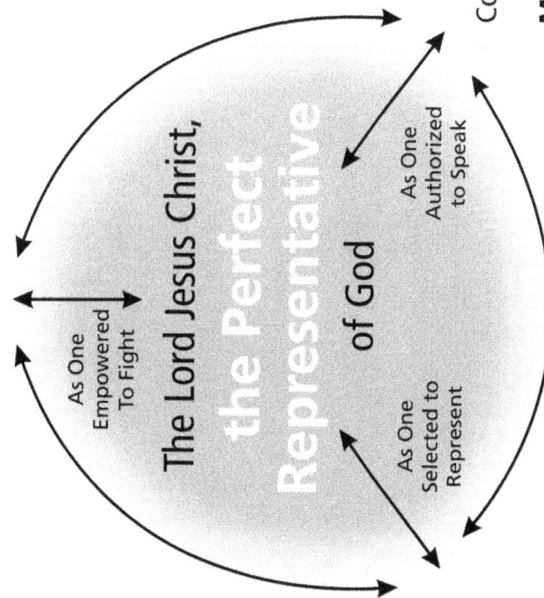

The Temptation of Jesus Christ
Challenge to and Contention with God's Rep

Mark 1.12-13 – The Spirit immediately drove him out into the wilderness. [13] *And he was in the wilderness forty days, being tempted by Satan. And he was with the wild animals, and the angels were ministering to him.*

Jesus Fulfills The Duties Of Being an Emissary

1. Receiving an *Assignment*, **John 10.17-18**

2. Resourced with an *Entrustment*, **John 3.34; Luke. 4.18**

3. Launched into *Engagement*, **John 5.30**

4. Answered with an *Assessment*, **Matthew 3.16-17**

5. New assignment after *Assessment*, **Philippians 2.9-11**

The Baptism of Jesus Christ
Commissioning and Confirmation of God's Rep

Mark 1.9-11 – *In those days Jesus came from Nazareth of Galilee and was baptized by John in the Jordan.* [10] And when he came up out of the water, immediately he saw the heavens opening and the Spirit descending on him like a dove. [11] And a voice came from heaven, "You are my beloved Son; with you I am well pleased."

The Public Preaching Ministry of Jesus Christ
Communication and Conveyance by God's Rep

Mark 1.14-15 – Now after John was arrested, Jesus came into Galilee, proclaiming the gospel of God, and saying, "The time is fulfilled, and the kingdom of God is at hand; repent and believe in the gospel."

The Lord Jesus Christ, **the Perfect Representative** of God

As One Empowered To Fight

As One Authorized to Speak

As One Selected to Represent

Appendix 27

Roles of Representational Leadership

Rev. Dr. Don L. Davis

Roles of Representational Leadership

| DEPUTY | SPOKESPERSON | MODEL | MESSENGER | AGENT |

Things that may or may not have any bearing on the personal representation of another:

Background

Experience

Competence

Confidence

Opinion of Others

Education

Majority Acceptance

Officials

Traditional Ways of Promotion and Demotion

Seniority

Voting Habits

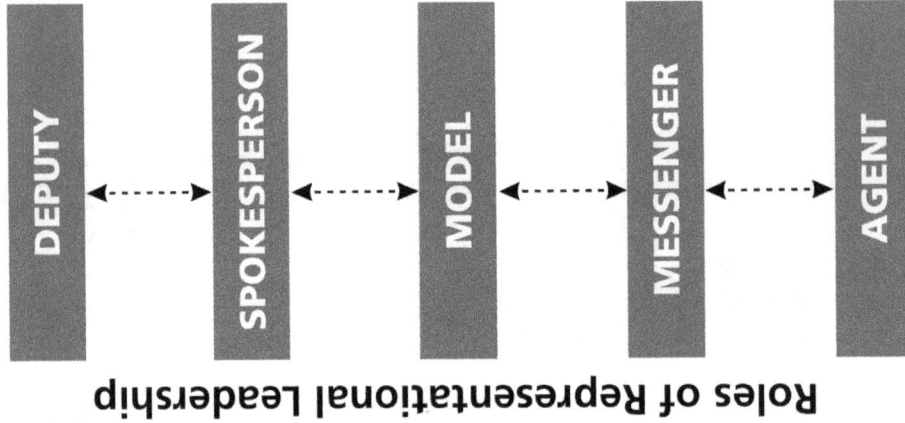

Has someone granted to you the right and responsibility to stand for them in this situation?

What precisely have you been authorized to do and entrusted to steward or accomplish on behalf of the person who granted these rights to you?

What is at stake in my faithful accomplishment of my entrusted status--what will I gain or what will I forfeit with this charge?

APPENDIX 28

Steps to Equipping Others

Rev. Dr. Don L. Davis

Step One

You become a Master at it, striving toward mastery by practicing it with regularity, excellence, and enjoyment. You must learn to do it, and do it excellently. While you need not be perfect, you should be able to do it, be doing it regularly, and growing in your practice of it. This is the most fundamental principle of all mentoring and discipling. You cannot teach what you do not know or cannot do, and when your Apprentice is fully trained, they will become like you (Luke 6.40).

Step Two

You select an Apprentice who also desires to develop mastery of the thing, one who is teachable, faithful, and available. Jesus called the Twelve to be with him, and to send them out to preach (Mark 3.14). His relationship was clear, neither vague nor coerced. The roles and responsibilities of the relationship must be carefully outlined, clearly discussed, and openly agreed upon.

Step Three

You instruct and model the task in the presence of and accompanied by your Apprentice. He/she comes alongside you to listen, observe, and watch. You do it with regularity and excellence, and your Apprentice comes along "for the ride," who is brought along to see how it is done. A picture is worth a thousand words. This sort of non-pressure participant observation is critical to in-depth training (2 Tim. 2.2; Phil. 4.9).

Step Four

You do the task and practice the thing together. Having modeled the act for your Apprentice in many ways and at many times, you now invite them to cooperate with you by becoming a partner-in-training, working together on the task. The goal is to do the task together, taking mutual responsibility. You coordinate your efforts, working together in harmony to accomplish the thing.

Step Five

Your Apprentice does the task on their own, in the presence of and accompanied by you. You provide opportunity to your Apprentice to practice the thing in your presence while you watch and listen. You make yourself available to help, but offer it in the background; you provide counsel, input, and guidance as they request it, but they do the task. Afterwards, you evaluate and clarify anything you may have observed as you accompanied your Apprentice (2 Cor. 11.1).

Step Six

*Your Apprentice does the thing solo, practicing it regularly, automatically, and excellently **until mastery of the thing is gained**.* After your Apprentice has done the task under your supervision excellently, he/she is ready to be released to make the thing his/her own by habituating the act in his/her own life. You are a co-doer with your Apprentice; both of you are doing the task without coercion or aid from the other. The goal is familiarity and skillfulness in the task (Heb. 5.11-15).

Step Seven

*Your Apprentice **becomes a Mentor of others**, selecting other faithful Apprentices to equip and train.* The training process bears fruit when the Apprentice, having mastered the thing you have equipped him/her to do, becomes a trainer of others. This is the heart of the discipling and training process (Heb. 5.11-14; 2 Tim. 2.2).

APPENDIX 29

The Nature of Dynamic Church Planting Movements:
Mapping the Elements of Effective Urban Mission

Rev. Dr. Don L. Davis

A Missional Appraisal of Dynamic Church Plant Movements				
Elements	**Shared Spirituality**	**People Group Identity**	**Dynamic Standardization**	**Level of Fruitfulness**
Term	Spiritual Formation	Contextualization	Multiplication	
Definition	Possessing a common spiritual identity in a church body that expresses the Great Tradition	Affirming our freedom in Christ to embody the faith within ethnicity and culture	Rapidly reproducing healthy churches of a kind through shared protocols and resources	
Explanation	Presumes a valid, distinctive apostolic spiritual identity embodied in a church body (why and what)	Conditions how that identity is understood, practiced (where and with whom)	Determines how that identity is formed, nourished, and multiplied (how)	
Burden	To express a common spiritual vision and discipline in shared practice	To contextualize within a culture or people group	To organize and coordinate resources for the common good	
Model 1	Cultivated identity built on spirituality and practice	Full attention to culture and ethnicity	Integrated structures and common protocols	Most Effective
Model 2	Shared elements of spirituality and practice	More attention to culture and ethnicity	Voluntary structures and optional protocols	More Effective
Model 3	Divergent, dissimilar spirituality and practice	Some attention to culture and ethnicity	Iconoclastic structures and divergent protocols	Less Effective
Model 4	Fragmented approaches to spirituality and practice	No attention to culture and ethnicity	Arbitrary structures and random protocols	Least Effective

(Models 1-4 listed under "Alternative Approaches in Church Planting")

History and Identity (*Our Common Heritage*)
Our church planting movements must anchor themselves in the Great Tradition while, at the same time, identify themselves within a church body which shares a common identity and history that all embrace, regardless of culture or ethnicity.

Membership and Belonging (*Our Common Discipline*)

Our church planting movements must be anchored in evangelical and historically orthodox presentations of the Gospel that results in conversions to Jesus Christ and incorporation into solid, healthy local churches.

Theology and Doctrine (*Our Common Faith*)

Our church planting movements must be anchored in a common theology and Christian education (catechism) that reflects a commonly-held faith rooted in the Great Tradition.

Worship and Liturgy (*Our Common Worship*)

Our church planting movements must share a hymnody, liturgy, symbology, and spiritual formation that enables them to worship and glorify God, and also challenges them to contextualize the faith in ways that attracts and appeals to urbanites.

Convocation and Association (*Our Common Partnership*)

Our church planting movements must seek to connect, link, and associate the congregations and leaders within our movements to one another in regular communication, fellowship, and partnership in mission.

Justice and Support Ministries (*Our Common Service*)

Our church planting movements must demonstrate the love and justice of the Kingdom in the city in practical ways that allow its congregations to love their neighbors as they love themselves.

Resources and Finances (*Our Common Stewardship*)

Our church planting movements must handle their financial affairs and resources with wise, streamlined, and reproducible policies that allow for the good management of our monies and goods.

Church Government (*Our Common Polity*)

Our church planting movements must be organized around a common polity, management, and governing policy that allow for efficient management of their opportunities and resources.

Leadership Development Policies and Strategies (*Our Common Shepherding*)

Our church planting movements must identify, equip, and support pastors and missionaries in our congregations that join our leaders to one another in faith and practice.

Evangelism and Missions (*Our Common Mission*)

Our church planting movements must coordinate their efforts and activities to give clear witness of Jesus in the city, resulting in planting significant numbers of new congregations who join our movements as quickly as possible.

APPENDIX 30

The Theology of Christus Victor

Rev. Dr. Don L. Davis

	The Promised Messiah	The Word Made Flesh	The Son of Man	The Suffering Servant	The Lamb of God	The Victorious Conqueror	The Reigning Lord in Heaven	The Bridegroom and Coming King
Biblical Framework	Israel's hope of Yahweh's anointed who would redeem his people	In the person of Jesus of Nazareth, the Lord has come to the world	As the promised king and divine Son of Man, Jesus reveals the Father's glory and salvation to the world	As Inaugurator of the Kingdom of God, Jesus demonstrates God's reign present through his words, wonders, and works	As both High Priest and Paschal Lamb, Jesus offers himself to God on our behalf as a sacrifice for sin	In his resurrection from the dead and ascension to God's right hand, Jesus is proclaimed as Victor over the power of sin and death	Now reigning at God's right hand till his enemies are made his footstool, Jesus pours out his benefits on his body	Soon the risen and ascended Lord will return to gather his Bride, the Church, and consummate his work
Scripture References	Isa. 9.6-7 Jer. 23.5-6 Isa. 11.1-10	John 1.14-18 Matt. 1.20-23 Phil. 2.6-8	Matt. 2.1-11 Num. 24.17 Luke 1.78-79	Mark 1.14-15 Matt. 12.25-30 Luke 17.20-21	2 Cor. 5.18-21 Isa. 52-53 John 1.29	Eph. 1.16-23 Phil. 2.5-11 Col. 1.15-20	1 Cor. 15.25 Eph. 4.15-16 Acts. 2.32-36	Rom. 14.7-9 Rev. 5.9-13 1 Thess. 4.13-18
Jesus' History	The pre-incarnate, only begotten Son of God in glory	His conception by the Spirit, and birth to Mary	His manifestation to the Magi and to the world	His teaching, exorcisms, miracles, and mighty works among the people	His suffering, crucifixion, death, and burial	His resurrection, with appearances to his witnesses, and his ascension to the Father	The sending of the Holy Spirit and his gifts, and Christ's session in heaven at the Father's right hand	His soon return from heaven to earth as Lord and Christ: the Second Coming
Description	The biblical promise for the seed of Abraham, the prophet like Moses, the son of David	In the Incarnation, God has come to us; Jesus reveals to humankind the Father's glory in fullness	In Jesus, God has shown his salvation to the entire world, including the Gentiles	In Jesus, the promised Kingdom of God has come visibly to earth, demonstrating his binding of Satan and rescinding the Curse	As God's perfect Lamb, Jesus offers himself up to God as a sin offering on behalf of the entire world	In his resurrection and ascension, Jesus destroyed death, disarmed Satan, and rescinded the Curse	Jesus is installed at the Father's right hand as Head of the Church, Firstborn from the dead, and supreme Lord in heaven	As we labor in his harvest field in the world, so we await Christ's return, the fulfillment of his promise
Church Year	Advent	Christmas	Season after Epiphany Baptism and Transfiguration	Lent	Holy Week Passion	Eastertide Easter, Ascension Day, Pentecost	Season after Pentecost Trinity Sunday	Season after Pentecost All Saints Day, Reign of Christ the King
Spiritual Formation	*The Coming of Christ* As we await his Coming, let us proclaim and affirm the hope of Christ	*The Birth of Christ* O Word made flesh, let us every heart prepare him room to dwell	*The Manifestation of Christ* Divine Son of Man, show the nations your salvation and glory	*The Ministry of Christ* In the person of Christ, the power of the reign of God has come to earth and to the Church	*The Suffering and Death of Christ* May those who share the Lord's death be resurrected with him	*The Resurrection and Ascension of Christ* Let us participate by faith in the victory of Christ over the power of sin, Satan, and death	*The Heavenly Session of Christ* Come, indwell us, Holy Spirit, and empower us to advance Christ's Kingdom in the world	*The Reign of Christ* We live and work in expectation of his soon return, seeking to please him in all things

APPENDIX 31

The Story of God: Our Sacred Roots

Rev. Dr. Don L. Davis

The Alpha and the Omega	Christus Victor	Come, Holy Spirit	Your Word Is Truth	The Great Confession	His Life in Us	Living in the Way	Reborn to Serve
The LORD God is the source, sustainer, and end of all things in the heavens and earth. All things were formed and exist by his will and for his eternal glory, the triune God, Father, Son, and Holy Spirit, Rom. 11.36.							
THE TRIUNE GOD'S UNFOLDING DRAMA — God's Self-Revelation in Creation, Israel, and Christ			THE CHURCH'S PARTICIPATION IN GOD'S UNFOLDING DRAMA — Fidelity to the Apostolic Witness to Christ and His Kingdom				
The Objective Foundation: The Sovereign Love of God — God's Narration of His Saving Work in Christ			The Subjective Practice: Salvation by Grace through Faith — The Redeemed's Joyous Response to God's Saving Work in Christ				
The Author of the Story	*The Champion of the Story*	*The Interpreter of the Story*	*The Testimony of the Story*	*The People of the Story*	*Re-enactment of the Story*	*Embodiment of the Story*	*Continuation of the Story*
The Father as *Director*	Jesus as *Lead Actor*	The Spirit as *Narrator*	Scripture as *Script*	As Saints, *Confessors*	As Worshipers, *Ministers*	As Followers, *Sojourners*	As Servants, *Ambassadors*
Christian *Worldview*	Communal *Identity*	Spiritual *Experience*	Biblical *Authority*	Orthodox *Theology*	Priestly *Worship*	Congregational *Discipleship*	Kingdom *Witness*
Theistic and *Trinitarian Vision*	Christ-centered *Foundation*	Spirit-Indwelt and -Filled Community	Canonical and *Apostolic Witness*	Ancient Creedal *Affirmation of Faith*	Weekly Gathering in Christian Assembly	Corporate, Ongoing Spiritual Formation	Active Agents of the Reign of God
Sovereign *Willing*	Messianic *Representing*	Divine *Comforting*	Inspired *Testifying*	Truthful *Retelling*	Joyful *Excelling*	Faithful *Indwelling*	Hopeful *Compelling*
Creator / True Maker of the Cosmos	Recapitulation / Typos and Fulfillment of the Covenant	Life-Giver / Regeneration and Adoption	Divine Inspiration / God-breathed Word	The Confession of Faith / Union with Christ	Song and Celebration / Historical Recitation	Pastoral Oversight / Shepherding the Flock	Explicit Unity / Love for the Saints
Owner / Sovereign Disposer of Creation	Revealer / Incarnation of the Word	Teacher / Illuminator of the Truth	Sacred History / Historical Record	Baptism into Christ / Communion of Saints	Homilies and Teachings / Prophetic Proclamation	Shared Spirituality / Common Journey through the Spiritual Disciplines	Radical Hospitality / Evidence of God's Kingdom Reign
Ruler / Blessed Controller of All Things	Redeemer / Reconciler of All Things	Helper / Endowment and the Power	Biblical Theology / Divine Commentary	The Rule of Faith / Apostles' Creed and Nicene Creed	The Lord's Supper / Dramatic Re-enactment	Embodiment / Anamnesis and Prolepsis through the Church Year	Extravagant Generosity / Good Works
Covenant Keeper / Faithful Promisor	Restorer / Christ, the Victor over the powers of evil	Guide / Divine Presence and Shekinah	Spiritual Food / Sustenance for the Journey	The Vincentian Canon / Ubiquity, antiquity, universality	Eschatological Foreshadowing / The Already/Not Yet	Effective Discipling / Spiritual Formation in the Believing Assembly	Evangelical Witness / Making Disciples of All People Groups

APPENDIX 32

There Is a River:
*Identifying the Streams of a Revitalized Authentic Christian Community in the City**

Rev. Dr. Don L. Davis

Ps. 46.4 (ESV) - There is a river whose streams make glad the city of God, the holy habitation of the Most High.

Tributaries of Authentic Historic Biblical Faith

Recognized Biblical Identity	Revived Urban Spirituality	Reaffirmed Historical Connectivity	Refocused Kingdom Authority
The Church Is One	*The Church Is Holy*	*The Church Is Catholic*	*The Church Is Apostolic*
A Call to Biblical Fidelity Recognizing the Scriptures as the anchor and foundation of the Christian faith and practice	**A Call to the Freedom, Power, and Fullness of the Holy Spirit** Walking in the holiness, power, gifting, and liberty of the Holy Spirit in the body of Christ	**A Call to Historic Roots and Continuity** Confessing the common historical identity and continuity of authentic Christian faith	**A Call to the Apostolic Faith** Affirming the apostolic tradition as the authoritative ground of the Christian hope
A Call to Messianic Kingdom Identity Rediscovering the story of the promised Messiah and his Kingdom in Jesus of Nazareth	**A Call to Live as Sojourners and Aliens as the People of God** Defining authentic Christian discipleship as faithful membership among God's people	**A Call to Affirm and Express the Global Communion of Saints** Expressing cooperation and collaboration with all other believers, both local and global	**A Call to Representative Authority** Submitting joyfully to God's gifted servants in the Church as undershepherds of true faith
A Call to Creedal Affinity Embracing the Nicene Creed as the shared rule of faith of historic orthodoxy	**A Call to Liturgical, Sacramental, and Catechetical Vitality** Walking in the holiness, power, gifting, and liberty of the Holy Spirit in the body of Christ	**A Call to Radical Hospitality and Good Works** Expressing kingdom love to all, and especially to those of the household of faith	**A Call to Prophetic and Holistic Witness** Proclaiming Christ and his Kingdom in word and deed to our neighbors and all peoples

* This schema is an adaptation and is based on the insights of the *Chicago Call* statement of May 1977, where various leading evangelical scholars and practitioners met to discuss the relationship of modern evangelicalism to the historic Christian faith.

APPENDIX 33

Traditions
(Paradosis)

Rev. Dr. Don L. Davis and Rev. Terry G. Cornett

> Remember the days of old; consider the years of many generations; ask your father, and he will show you, your elders, and they will tell you.
>
> ~ Deuteronomy 32.7

Strong's Definition
Paradosis. Transmission, i.e. (concretely) a precept; specifically, the Jewish traditionary law

Vine's Explanation
Denotes "a tradition," and hence, by metonymy, (a) "the teachings of the rabbis," . . .(b) "apostolic teaching," . . . of instructions concerning the gatherings of believers, of Christian doctrine in general . . . of instructions concerning everyday conduct.

I. **The concept of tradition in Scripture is rooted in the remembrance, celebration, enactment, and proclamation of the story of God's promise to redeem and save a people for his own.**

Every age of Christian testimony has given witness to their deep faith and hope in the salvation promise of the triune God to redeem a people out of the world for his own possession and service. The history of the Judeo-Christian faith is anchored in a hope which is renewed daily, weekly, monthly, and annually in the worship and service of the people of God. This hope is rooted in the work of Jesus of Nazareth, demonstrated in his perfect life, expressed in his death on the Cross, and vindicated by his resurrection from the dead and ascension to the Father's right hand. Rooted in the historical journey of God's people Israel, and made real in the life and service of the Church, tradition involves those acts, behaviors, customs, and practices which articulate, celebrate, enact, retell, defend, and embody the story of God's salvation in Jesus, those doctrines and practices whereby we sanctify the present by remembering the past so we can better live in light of the future, our true hope of glory in Christ.

Exod. 12.24-27 – "You shall observe this rite as a statute for you and for your sons forever. And when you come to the land that the Lord will give you, as he has promised, you shall keep this service. And when your children say to you, 'What do you mean by this service?' you shall say, 'It is the sacrifice of the Lord's Passover, for he passed over the houses of the people of Israel in Egypt, when he struck the Egyptians but spared our houses.'" And the people bowed their heads and worshiped.

Jer. 6.16 – Thus says the Lord: "Stand by the roads, and look, and ask for the ancient paths, where the good way is; and walk in it, and find rest for your souls. But they said, 'We will not walk in it'" (cf. Exod. 3.15; Judg. 2.17; 1 Kings 8.57-58; Ps. 78.1-6).

Deut. 26.5-11 – And you shall make response before the Lord your God, "A wandering Aramean was my father. And he went down into Egypt and sojourned there, few in number, and there he became a nation, great, mighty, and populous. And the Egyptians treated us harshly and humiliated us and laid on us hard labor. Then we cried to the Lord, the God of our fathers, and the Lord heard our voice and saw our affliction, our toil, and our oppression. And the Lord brought us out of Egypt with a mighty hand and an outstretched arm, with great deeds of terror, with signs and wonders. And he brought us into this place and gave us this land, a land flowing with milk and honey. And behold, now I bring the first of the fruit of the ground, which you, O Lord, have given me." And you shall set it down before the Lord your God and worship before the Lord your God. And you shall rejoice in all the good that the Lord your God has given to you and to your house, you, and the Levite, and the sojourner who is among you.

Exod. 13.8-9 – You shall tell your son on that day, "It is because of what the Lord did for me when I came out of Egypt." And it shall be to you as a sign on your hand and as a memorial between your eyes, that the law of the Lord may be in your mouth. For with a strong hand the Lord has brought you out of Egypt.

2 Chron. 35.25 (NIV) – Jeremiah composed laments for Josiah, and to this day all the men and women singers commemorate Josiah in the laments. These became a tradition in Israel and are written in the Laments (cf. Gen. 32.32; Judg. 11.38-40).

II. Godly tradition edifies, grounds, and reinforces the truth and story of God in our lives. However, because of sinful habits and dead orthodoxy, not all tradition is godly.

Any individual tradition must be judged by its faithfulness to the Word of God and its usefulness in helping people maintain obedience to Christ's example and teaching.* In the Gospels, Jesus frequently rebukes the Pharisees for establishing traditions that nullify rather than uphold God's commands.

Mark 7.8 – "You leave the commandment of God and hold to the tradition of men" (cf. Matt. 15.2-6; Mark. 7.13).

Col. 2.8 – See to it that no one takes you captive by philosophy and empty deceit, according to human tradition, according to the elemental spirits of the world, and not according to Christ.

III. Without the fullness of the Holy Spirit among the people of God, the constant edification of the Scripture, and the passionate remembrance and celebration of God's works in history, tradition will inevitably lead to dead formalism.

Those who are spiritual are filled with the Holy Spirit, whose power and leading alone provides individuals and congregations a sense of freedom and vitality in all they practice and believe. However, when the practices and teachings of any given tradition are no longer infused by the power of the Holy Spirit and the Word of God, tradition loses its effectiveness, and may actually become counterproductive to our discipleship in Jesus Christ.

Eph. 5.18 – And do not get drunk with wine, for that is debauchery, but be filled with the Spirit.

Gal. 5.22-25 – But the fruit of the Spirit is love, joy, peace, patience, kindness, goodness, faithfulness, gentleness, self-control; against such things there is no law. And those who belong to Christ Jesus have crucified the flesh with its passions and desires. If we live by the Spirit, let us also walk by the Spirit.

2 Cor. 3.5-6 – Not that we are sufficient in ourselves to claim anything as coming from us, but our sufficiency is from God, who has made us competent to be ministers of a new covenant, not of the letter but of the Spirit. For the letter kills, but the Spirit gives life.

IV. Fidelity and reproduction to the Apostolic tradition (i.e., the testimony, teaching, and ethical vision of Christ and his kingdom) is the essence of Christian maturity.

Tradition for the Church is not misguided nor arbitrary. Rather, we draw our sense of identity and history from the story of Jesus of Nazareth based on the eyewitness testimony of the apostles, and their commentary and explanation of the meaning of the Christ event for our lives. The Church is a *messianic hermeneutical community*, drawing its life from its conviction, proclamation, celebration, and demonstration of the meaning of the person and work of Jesus as embodied in the history of Israel, as demonstrated through his incarnation and passion, and verified in his resurrection and ascension to the right hand of God. Their bold, clear proclamation of his coming again to complete his work on the Cross and to establish the reign of God in this world is the Church's hope and love. As so often said in the African American Christian worship communities, tradition makes this story and its hope "plain," telling to all in worship, ritual, celebration, and lifestyle that Jesus of Nazareth is the Chosen One of God, borne witness to by the apostles. Embracing and defending their witness is the heart of Christian maturity and discipleship.

2 Tim. 2.2 – and what you have heard from me in the presence of many witnesses entrust to faithful men who will be able to teach others also.

1 Cor. 11.1-2 – Be imitators of me, as I am of Christ. Now I commend you because you remember me in everything and maintain the traditions even as I delivered them to you (cf.1 Cor. 4.16-17; 2 Tim. 1.13-14; 2 Thess. 3.7-9; Phil. 4.9).

1 Cor. 15.3-8 – For I delivered to you as of first importance what I also received: that Christ died for our sins in accordance with the Scriptures, that he was buried, that he was raised on the third day in accordance with the Scriptures, and that he appeared to Cephas, then to the twelve. Then he appeared to more than five hundred brothers at one time, most of whom are still alive, though some have fallen asleep. Then he appeared to James, then to all the apostles. Last of all, as to one untimely born, he appeared also to me.

V. The Apostle Paul often includes to the churches an appeal to the tradition for support in both doctrinal and ethical practices.

The apostolic tradition was the yardstick and plumb line of authentic faith, genuine Christian love, and authentic demonstration of Christian hope in the church's faith and practice.

1 Cor. 11.16 – If anyone is inclined to be contentious, we have no such practice, nor do the churches of God (cf. 1 Cor. 1.2; 7.17; 15.3).

1 Cor. 14.33-34 – For God is not a God of confusion but of peace. As in all the churches of the saints, the women should keep silent in the churches. For they are not permitted to speak, but should be in submission, as the Law also says.

VI. When a congregation uses received tradition to remain faithful to the "Word of God," they are commended by the apostles.

The apostles not only expected the churches to receive the traditions of faith and practice that they had given to the people of God, they were instructed to maintain and defend them, to hold fast to what they have been given, and to stand firm upon it for what it truly was, the authoritative word of God.

1 Cor. 11.2 – Now I commend you because you remember me in everything and maintain the traditions even as I delivered them to you.

2 Thess. 2.15 – So then, brothers, stand firm and hold to the traditions that you were taught by us, either by our spoken word or by our letter.

2 Thess. 3.6 – Now we command you, brothers, in the name of our Lord Jesus Christ, that you keep away from any brother who is walking in idleness and not in accord with the tradition that you received from us.

The Founders of Tradition: Three Levels of Christian Authority

Exod. 3.15 (ESV) – God also said to Moses, "Say this to the people of Israel, 'The Lord, the God of your fathers, the God of Abraham, the God of Isaac, and the God of Jacob, has sent me to you.' This is my name forever, and thus I am to be remembered throughout all generations."

I. The Authoritative Tradition: The Apostles and the Prophets (The Holy Scriptures)

> So then you are no longer strangers and aliens, but you are fellow citizens with the saints and members of the household of God, built on the foundation of the apostles and prophets, Christ Jesus himself being the cornerstone, in whom the whole structure, being joined together, grows into a holy temple in the Lord.
>
> ~ The Apostle Paul (Ephesians 2.19-21)

Those who gave eyewitness testimony to the revelation and saving acts of Yahweh, first in Israel, and ultimately in Jesus Christ the Messiah. This testimony is binding for all people, at all times, and in all places. It is the authoritative tradition by which all subsequent tradition is judged.

See below, Defining the Great Tradition.

II. The Great Tradition: The Ecumenical Councils and their Creeds*

> What has been believed everywhere, always, and by all.
>
> ~ Vincent of Lerins

The Great Tradition is the core dogma (doctrine) of the church. It represents the teaching of the Church as it has understood the Authoritative Tradition (the Holy Scriptures), and summarizes those essential truths that Christians of all ages have confessed and believed. To these doctrinal statements the whole church, (Catholic, Orthodox, and Protestant)** gives its assent. The worship and theology of the church reflects this core dogma, which finds its summation and fulfillment in the person and work of Jesus Christ. From earliest times, Christians have expressed their devotion to God in its church calendar, a yearly pattern of worship which summarizes and reenacts the events of Christ's life.

** Even the more radical wing of the Protestant reformation (Anabaptists) who were the most reluctant to embrace the creeds as dogmatic instruments of faith, did not disagree with the essential content found in them. "They assumed the Apostolic Creed – they called it 'The Faith,' Der Glaube, as did most people." See John Howard Yoder, *Preface to Theology: Christology and Theological Method*, (Grand Rapids: Brazos Press, 2002), pp. 222-223.

III. Specific Church Traditions: The Founders of Denominations and Orders

> The Presbyterian Church (U.S.A.) has approximately 2.5 million members, 11,200 congregations and 21,000 ordained ministers. Presbyterians trace their history to the 16th century and the Protestant Reformation. Our heritage, and much of what we believe, began with the French lawyer John Calvin (1509-1564), whose writings crystallized much of the Reformed thinking that came before him.
>
> ~ The Presbyterian Church, U.S.A.

Christians have expressed their faith in Jesus Christ in various ways through specific movements and traditions which embrace and express the Authoritative Tradition and the Great Tradition in unique ways. For instance, Catholic movements have arisen around people like Benedict, Francis, or Dominic, and among Protestants people like Martin Luther, John Calvin, Ulrich Zwingli, and John Wesley. Women have founded vital movements of Christian faith (e.g., Aimee Semple McPherson of the Foursquare Church), as well as minorities (e.g., Richard Allen of the African Methodist Episcopal Church or Charles H. Mason of the Church of God in Christ, who also helped to spawn the Assemblies of God), all which attempted to express the Authoritative Tradition and the Great Tradition in a specific way consistent with their time and expression.

The emergence of vital, dynamic movements of the faith at different times and among different peoples reveal the fresh working of the Holy Spirit throughout history. Thus, inside Catholicism, new communities have arisen such as the Benedictines, Franciscans, and Dominicans; and outside Catholicism, new denominations have emerged (Lutherans, Presbyterians, Methodists, Church of God in Christ, etc.). Each of these specific traditions have "founders," key leaders whose energy and vision helped to establish a unique expression of Christian faith and practice. Of course, to be legitimate, these movements must adhere to and faithfully express both the Authoritative Tradition and the Great Tradition. Members of these specific traditions embrace their own unique practices and patterns of spirituality, but these unique features are not necessarily binding on the church at large. They represent the unique expressions of that community's understanding of and faithfulness to the Authoritative and Great Traditions.

Specific traditions seek to express and live out this faithfulness to the Authoritative and Great Traditions through their worship, teaching, and service. They seek to make the Gospel clear within new cultures or sub-cultures, speaking and modeling the hope of Christ into new situations shaped by their own set of questions posed in light of their own unique circumstances. These movements, therefore, seek to contextualize the Authoritative tradition in a way that faithfully and effectively leads new groups of people to faith in Jesus Christ, and incorporates those who believe into the community of faith that obeys his teachings and gives witness of him to others.

Defining the "Great Tradition"

The Great Tradition (sometimes called the "classical Christian tradition") is defined by Robert E. Webber as follows:

> [It is] the broad outline of Christian belief and practice developed from the Scriptures between the time of Christ and the middle of the fifth century.
>
> ~ Robert E. Webber. *The Majestic Tapestry*. Nashville: Thomas Nelson Publishers, 1986, p. 10.

This tradition is widely affirmed by Protestant theologians both ancient and modern.

> Thus those ancient Councils of Nicea, Constantinople, the first of Ephesus, Chalcedon, and the like, which were held for refuting errors, we willingly embrace, and reverence as sacred, in so far as relates to doctrines of faith, for they contain nothing but the pure and genuine interpretation of Scripture, which the holy Fathers with spiritual prudence adopted to crush the enemies of religion who had then arisen.
>
> ~ John Calvin. *Institutes*, IV, ix. 8

> …most of what is enduringly valuable in contemporary biblical exegesis was discovered by the fifth century.
>
> ~ Thomas C. Oden. *The Word of Life*. San Francisco: HarperSanFrancisco, 1989, p. xi

> The first four Councils are by far the most important, as they settled the orthodox faith on the Trinity and the Incarnation.
>
> ~ Philip Schaff. *The Creeds of Christendom, v. 1*. Grand Rapids: Baker Book House, 1996, p. 44.

Our reference to the Ecumenical Councils and Creeds is, therefore, focused on those Councils which retain a widespread agreement in the church among Catholics, Orthodox, *and Protestants*. While Catholic and Orthodox share common agreement on the first seven councils, Protestants tend to affirm and use primarily the first four. Therefore, those councils which *continue to be shared by the whole church* are completed with the Council of Chalcedon in 451.

It is worth noting that each of these four Ecumenical Councils took place in a pre-European cultural context and that none of them were held in Europe. They were councils of the whole church and they reflected a time in which Christianity was primarily an eastern religion in it's geographic core. By modern reckoning, their participants were African, Asian, and European. The councils reflected a church that ". . . has roots in cultures far distant from Europe and preceded the development of modern European identity, and [of which] some of its greatest minds have been African" (Oden, *The Living God*, SanFrancisco: HarperSanFrancisco, 1987, p. 9).

Perhaps the most important achievement of the Councils was the creation of what is now commonly called the Nicene Creed. It serves as a summary statement of the Christian faith that can be agreed on by Catholic, Orthodox, and Protestant Christians.

The first four Ecumenical Councils are summarized in the chart on the following page.

Name/Date/Location	Purpose		
First Ecumenical Council 325 A.D *Nicea, Asia Minor*	Defending against:	*Arianism*	
	Question answered:	*Was Jesus God?*	
	Action:	*Developed the initial form of the Nicene Creed to serve as a summary of the Christian faith*	
Second Ecumenical Council 381 A.D *Constantinople, Asia Minor*	Defending against:	*Macedonianism*	
	Question answered:	*Is the Holy Spirit a personal and equal part of the Godhead?*	
	Action:	*Completed the Nicene Creed by expanding the article dealing with the Holy Spirit*	
Third Ecumenical Council 431 A.D *Ephesus, Asia Minor*	Defending against:	*Nestorianism*	
	Question answered:	*Is Jesus Christ both God and man in one person?*	
	Action:	*Defined Christ as the incarnate Word of God and affirmed his mother Mary as theotokos (God-bearer)*	
Fourth Ecumenical Council 451 A.D *Chalcedon, Asia Minor*	Defending against:	*Monophysitism*	
	Question answered:	*How can Jesus be both God and man?*	
	Action:	*Explained the relationship between Jesus's two natures (human and Divine)*	

Appendix 34

The Oikos Factor: Spheres of Relationship and Influence

Rev. Dr. Don L. Davis

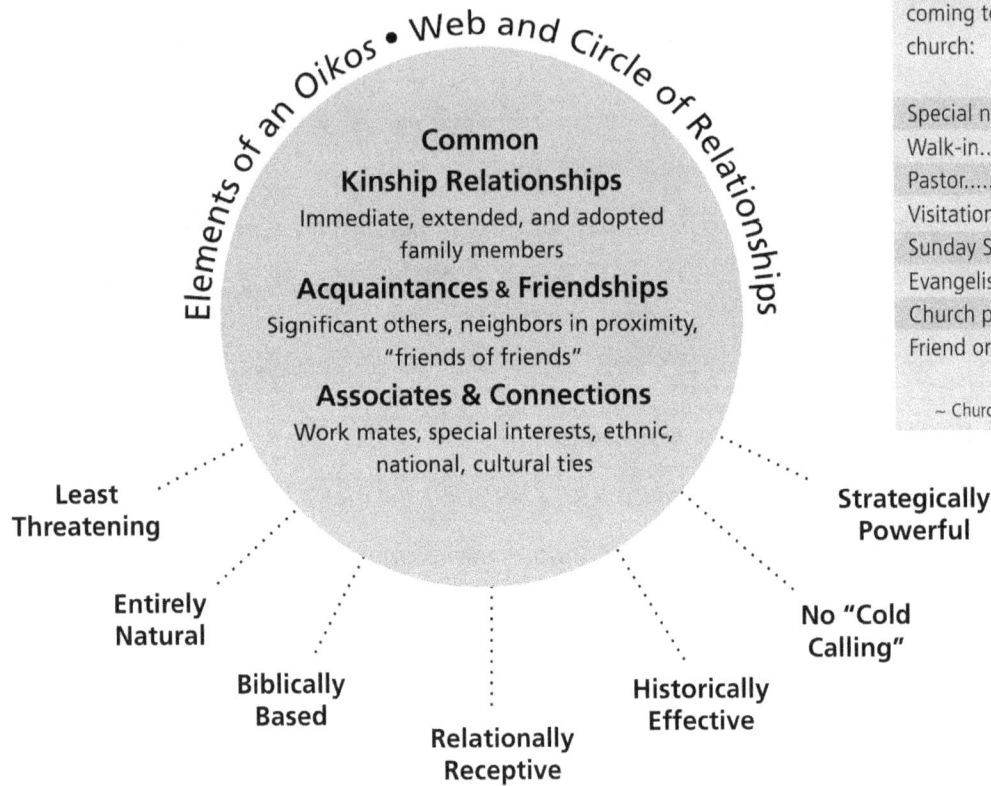

Elements of an Oikos • Web and Circle of Relationships

Common Kinship Relationships
Immediate, extended, and adopted family members

Acquaintances & Friendships
Significant others, neighbors in proximity, "friends of friends"

Associates & Connections
Work mates, special interests, ethnic, national, cultural ties

Least Threatening

Entirely Natural

Biblically Based

Relationally Receptive

Historically Effective

No "Cold Calling"

Strategically Powerful

Survey: 42,000 asked: Who or what was responsible for your coming to Christ and your church:

Special need	1-2%
Walk-in	2-3%
Pastor	5-6%
Visitation	1-2%
Sunday School	4-5%
Evangelistic crusade/TV	1/2%
Church program	2-3%
Friend or relative	75-90%!!

~ Church Growth, Inc. Monrovia, CA

Oikos (household) in the OT

"A household usually contained four generations, including men, married women, unmarried daughters, slaves of both sexes, persons without citizenship, and 'sojourners,' or resident foreign workers."

~ Hans Walter Wolff, Anthology of the Old Testament.

Oikos (household) in the NT

Evangelism and disciple making in our NT narratives are often described as following the flow of the relational networks of various people within their *oikoi* (households), that is, those natural lines of connection in which they resided and lived (c.f., Mark 5.19; Luke 19.9; John 4.53; 1.41-45, etc.). Andrew to Simon (John 1.41-45), and both Cornelius (Acts 10-11) and the Philippian jailer (Acts 16) are notable cases of evangelism and discipling through *oikoi*.

Oikos (household) among the urban poor

While great differences exist between cultures, kinship relationships, special interest groups, and family structures among urban populations, it is clear that urbanites connect with others far more on the basis of connections through relationships, friendships, and family than through proximity and neighborhood alone. Often times the closest friends of urban poor dwellers are not immediately close by in terms of neighborhood; family and friends may dwell blocks, even miles away. Taking the time to study the precise linkages of relationships among the dwellers in a certain area can prove extremely helpful in determining the most effective strategies for evangelism and disciple making in inner city contexts.

APPENDIX 35
Urban Church Planting:
A Topical Bibliography

Rev. Dr. Don L. Davis and Dr. Hank Voss

> You should read twenty-five percent of your books from the first 1,500 years of church history, twenty-five percent from the last 500 years, twenty-five percent from the last 100 years, and twenty-five percent from recent years.
>
> ~ Rick Warren, 2010

> It has always therefore been one of my main endeavors as a teacher to persuade the young that firsthand knowledge is not only more worth acquiring than second-hand knowledge, but is usually much easier and more delightful to acquire. . . . It is a good rule, after reading a new book, never to allow yourself another new one till you have read an old one in between. If that is too much for you, you should at least read one old one to every three new ones.
>
> ~ C. S. Lewis, 1944

I. Endear: A Church Planter Loves God with All of His Heart

This manual is dedicated to Rev. Bob Engel, a faithful and fervent church planter. Rev Engel has served as an example to many of one who is "endeared" to Christ. Early in his work as a church planter, Rev. Engel came across a list of "Spiritual Classics" from a pastor named A. W. Tozer. Tozer grew up extremely poor and was only able to formally complete a fifth grade education. He eventually became an influential pastor in Chicago, but more importantly, he was known as a man passionately in *Pursuit of God*. When asked how he remained so passionate for God, Tozer pointed to his "teachers." These teachers were the authors of some 25 spiritual classics that had helped to shape his *Knowledge of the Holy*.

Rev. Engel recommended this list to me (Hank) more than a decade ago as one place to start for those interested in deepening their exposure to some of the giants of the faith. Most of the books on this list are over a hundred years old, some more than a thousand. They have proved valuable across generations, and much of their content is rooted in the Great Tradition. Church Planters will need to read with discernment, but for those willing to invest the time, there is much spiritual profit to be mined from these sacred roots. Many of these books are available for free as downloads at *www.ccel.org*. Since most of these books have been reprinted by dozens of publishers, only the authors and titles are listed below.

1. *The Dark Night of the Soul*, by John of the Cross

2. *Practice of the Presence of God*, by Brother Lawrence

3. *A Testament of Devotion*, by Thomas Kelly

4. *Introduction to the Devout Life*, by Francis of Sales

5. *The Imitation of Christ*, by Thomas a Kempis

6. *Confessions*, by Augustine

7. *Private Devotions*, by Lancelot Andrewes

8. *Adornment of the Spiritual Marriage*, by Jan van Ruysbroeck

9. *Amendment of Life*, by Richard Rolle

10. *The Ascent of Mt. Carmel*, by John of the Cross

11. *The Ascent of Mt. Zion*, by Berdardeno de Laredo

12. *Book of Eternal Wisdom*, by Henry Suso

13. *Centuries of Meditations*, by Thomas Traherne

14. *Christian Perfection*, by Fenelon

15. *The Cloud of Unknowing*, Anonymous

16. *The Goad of Love*, by Walter Hilton

17. *A Guide to True Peace*, by Molinos and others

18. *Hymns*, by Gerhard Tersteegen

19. *Letters of Direction*, by de Tourville

20. *On the Incarnation*, by Athanasius

21. *On the Love of God*, by Bernard of Clairvaux

22. *Poems*, by Frederick Faber

23. *Poems*, by Isaac Watts

24. *Proslogium*, by Anselm

25. *The Quiet Way*, by Gerhard Tersteegen

26. *Revelations of Divine Love*, by Julian of Norwich

27. *The Scale of Perfection*, by Walter Hilton

28. *Sermons*, by John Tauler

29. *Song of Songs*, by Bernard of Clairvaux

30. *The Spiritual Combat*, by Lorenzo Scupoli

31. *The Spiritual Guide*, by Michael Molinos

32. *Talks of Instruction*, by Meister Eckhart

33. *Theologia Germanica* (Winkworth translation), Anonymous

34. *The Vision of God*, by Nicholas of Cusa

35. *The Way of Christ*, by Jacob Boehme

There are many other lists of spiritual classics available for those interested in exploring the deep mines of the spiritual writings of the Great Tradition. Other lists of spiritual classics and introductions to their contents can be found in the volumes below.

Bernhard M Christensen. *The Inward Pilgrimage: An Introduction to Christian Spiritual Classics*, Rev. ed. Minneapolis: Augsburg, 1996.

Edward Donnelly, ed. *You Must Read: Books That Have Shaped Our Lives*. Carlisle, PA: Banner of Truth Trust, 2015.

Arthur Holder, ed. *Christian Spirituality: The Classics*. New York: Routledge, 2010.

Eugene Peterson. *Take and Read: Spiritual Reading: An Annotated List*. Grand Rapids: Eerdmans, 1995.

II. TUMI Resources

In general, there are few resources designed explicitly for church planters working among the urban poor. The Urban Ministry Institute provides one exception to this general rule. Between 1995 and 2015 more than fifty books, training courses, and booklets have been published to resource those working among the poor. The resources listed below are relevant to both church planting and to the continued growth and health of urban churches serving the poor. Those specifically focused on the topic of church planting are marked with an asterisk.

A. Select Books

Don Davis. *Black and Human: Rediscovering King as a Resource for Black Theology and Ethics*. [Orig. 2000]. Wichita, KS: TUMI Press, 2015.

————. *Let God Arise! A Sober Call to Prevailing Prayer for a Dynamic Spiritual Awakening and the Aggressive Advancement of the Kingdom in America's Inner Cities*. Wichita, KS: The Urban Ministry Institute Press, 2000.*

————. *Leading and Feeding Urban Church Plant Teams*, 2nd ed. Wichita, KS: The Urban Ministry Institute Press, 2007.*

————. *For the Next Generation: The Urban Ministry Institute Mentor Manual*, 2nd ed. Wichita, KS: The Urban Ministry Institute Press, 2008.

————. *Sacred Roots: A Primer on Retrieving the Great Tradition*. Wichita, KS: The Urban Ministry Institute Press, 2010.*

————. *Multiplying Laborers for the Urban Harvest: Shifting the Paradigm for Servant Leadership Education*, 15th ed. Wichita, KS: The Urban Ministry Institute Press, 2013.

————. *The SIAFU Network Guidebook: Standing Together for Christ in the City*. Wichita, KS: The Urban Ministry Institute Press, 2013.

Dr. Don L. Davis, ed. *Planting Churches among the City's Poor: An Anthology of Urban Church Planting Resources*. Wichita, KS: The Urban Ministry Institute Press, 2015. 2 Volumes.*

Rev. Don Allsman and Dr. Don L. Davis. *Fight the Good Fight of Faith: Playing Your Part in God's Unfolding Drama*. Wichita, KS: The Urban Ministry Institute Press, 2015.

Don Allsman, Don L. Davis, and Hank Voss, eds. *Ripe for Harvest: A Guidebook for Planting Healthy Churches in the City*. Wichita, KS: TUMI Press, 2015.*

B. Select Published Courses and Curriculum Resources

Much of TUMI's emphasis has focused on producing resources easily accessible to urban leaders with a low level of literacy. Nearly all of the resources in this section of the bibliography include audio or video instructional content representing hundreds of hours of lectures designed to equip urban church leaders for ministry in their own context.

Don L. Davis. *Nurturing an Apostolic Heart* (Foundations for Ministry Series). Wichita, KS: The Urban Ministry Institute Press, 2000.*

———. *The Gospel of John* (Foundations for Ministry Series). Wichita, KS: The Urban Ministry Institute Press, 2002.

———. *The Kingdom of God*, vol. 2, 16 vols. (The Capstone Curriculum). Wichita, KS: The Urban Ministry Institute Press, 2004.

———. *Bible Interpretation*, vol. 5, 16 vols. (The Capstone Curriculum). Wichita, KS: The Urban Ministry Institute Press, 2005.

———. *Conversion and Calling,* vol. 1, 16 vols. (The Capstone Curriculum). Wichita, KS: The Urban Ministry Institute Press, 2005.

———. *Doing Justice and Loving Mercy*, vol. 16, 16 vols. (The Capstone Curriculum). Wichita, KS: The Urban Ministry Institute Press, 2005.

———. *Evangelism and Spiritual Warfare*, vol. 8, 16 vols. (The Capstone Curriculum). Wichita, KS: The Urban Ministry Institute Press, 2005.*

———. *Focus on Reproduction*, vol. 12, 16 vols. (The Capstone Curriculum). Wichita, KS: The Urban Ministry Institute Press, 2005.*

———. *Foundations for Christian Mission*, vol. 4, 16 vols. (The Capstone Curriculum). Wichita, KS: The Urban Ministry Institute Press, 2005.*

———. *Foundations of Christian Leadership*, vol. 7, 16 vols. (The Capstone Curriculum). Wichita, KS: The Urban Ministry Institute Press, 2005.

———. *God the Father*, vol. 6, 16 vols. (The Capstone Curriculum). Wichita, KS: The Urban Ministry Institute Press, 2005.

———. *God the Son*, vol. 10, 16 vols. (The Capstone Curriculum). Wichita, KS: The Urban Ministry Institute Press, 2005.

———. *New Testament Witness to Christ and His Kingdom*, vol. 13, 16 vols. (The Capstone Curriculum). Wichita, KS: The Urban Ministry Institute Press, 2005.

———. *Old Testament Witness to Christ and His Kingdom*, vol. 9, 16 vols. (The Capstone Curriculum). Wichita, KS: The Urban Ministry Institute Press, 2005.

———. *Practicing Christian Leadership*, vol. 11, 16 vols. (The Capstone Curriculum). Wichita, KS: The Urban Ministry Institute Press, 2005.

———. *The Equipping Ministry*, vol. 15, 16 vols. (The Capstone Curriculum). Wichita, KS: The Urban Ministry Institute Press, 2005.

———. *A Compelling Testimony: Maintaining a Disciplined Walk, Christlike Character, and Godly Relationships as God's Servant* (Foundations for Ministry Series). Wichita, KS: The Urban Ministry Institute Press, 2006.

———. *A Biblical Vision, Part I: Mastering the Old Testament Witness to Christ and His Kingdom* (Foundations for Ministry Series). Wichita, KS: The Urban Ministry Institute Press, 2006.

———. *A Biblical Vision, Part II: Mastering the New Testament Witness to Christ and His Kingdom* (Foundations for Ministry Series). Wichita, KS: The Urban Ministry Institute Press, 2006.

———. *Winning the World: Facilitating Urban Church Planting Movements* (Foundations for Ministry Series). Wichita, KS: The Urban Ministry Institute Press, 2007.*

———. *Church Matters: Retrieving the Great Tradition* (Foundations for Ministry Series). Wichita, KS: The Urban Ministry Institute, 2007.*

———. *An Authentic Calling: Representing Christ and His Kingdom through the Church* (Foundations for Ministry Series). Wichita, KS: The Urban Ministry Institute Press, 2008.

———. *Master the Bible: How to Get and Keep the Big Picture of the Bible's Story* (Foundations for Ministry Series). Wichita, KS: The Urban Ministry Institute Press, 2008.

———. *Marking Time: Forming Spirituality through the Church Year* (Foundations for Ministry Series). Wichita, KS: The Urban Ministry Institute Press, 2009.

———. *Sacred Roots Workshop: Retrieving the Great Tradition in the Contemporary Church* (Foundations for Ministry Series). Wichita, KS: The Urban Ministry Institute Press, 2010.

———. *Ministry in a Multicultural and Unchurched Society* (Foundations for Ministry Series). Wichita, KS: The Urban Ministry Institute Press, 2012.

Don L. Davis and Terry G. Cornett. *Theology of the Church*, vol. 3, 16 vols. (The Capstone Curriculum). Wichita, KS: The Urban Ministry Institute Press, 2005.

Don L. Davis and Lorna Rasmussen, *Managing Projects for Ministry* (Foundations for Ministry Series). Wichita, KS: The Urban Ministry Institute Press, 2012.

Don L. Davis. *Church Resource CD*. Wichita, KS: The Urban Ministry Institute Press, 1999.

Don Davis and Don Allsman, eds. *The John Mark Curriculum.* Los Angeles: World Impact, 2000.*

C. Select Chapters, Articles, Shorter Works

Don L. Davis, "An Interview with Cornel West." *Iowa Journal of Cultural Studies* 12 (1993): 8–17.

———. "Overview and Framework for Church Planting Activity". Wichita, KS: The Urban Ministry Institute Press, 2000.*

———. *Making Joyful Noises: Mastering the Fundamentals of Music.* Wichita, KS: The Urban Ministry Institute Press, 2000.

———. "Creedal Theology: A Blueprint for Urban Leadership Momentum," in *Gaining Momentum: The Urban Ministry Institute Satellite Summit Workbook.* Wichita, KS: The Urban Ministry Institute Press, 2006, 77–94.

———. "Fleshing out the Universal Priesthood: Recommended Order for Morning and Evening Sacrifices to God," in *The Wondrous Cross: TUMI Annual 2009-2010.* Wichita, KS: The Urban Ministry Institute Press, 2009, 425–36.

———. *The Most Amazing Story Ever Told.* Wichita, KS: The Urban Ministry Institute Press, 2011.

———. *The SIAFU Network Chapter Meeting Guide: How to Inspire Souls and Transform Hearts through Your SIAFU Gathering.* Wichita, KS: The Urban Ministry Institute Press, 2013.

Terry Cornett and Don Davis. *Empowering People for Freedom, Wholeness, and Justice: Theological and Ethical Foundations for World Impact's Development Ministries.* Wichita, KS: The Urban Ministry Institute Press, 1996.

Carl Ellis, ed. with Don Davis and Pastor R. C. Smith. *Saving Our Sons: Confronting the Lure of Islam With Truth, Faith & Courage* (Chicago, IMANI Books, 2007).

Hank Voss. "Twenty Five Years of Church Planting Among the Poor: A Report," in *Planting Churches among the City's Poor: An Anthology of Urban Church Planting Resources, Vol. 1.* Ed. Don L. Davis. Wichita, KS: TUMI Press, 2015. pp. 471–510.

III. "Urban Ministry" and Church Planting among the Poor

World Impact has identified three expressions of the church for strategic purposes. These three expressions require different types of planters, resources, and strategic plans. All three expressions can be healthy representations of Christ's kingdom in urban neighborhoods. The first expression is the Small ("House") Church. These churches are gatherings of 20-50 people for smaller expressions of the body of Christ in a local neighborhood. The second expression is the Community ("Storefront") Church. These churches range between 50 and 200 people and are among the most common expression of the church found in North America today. The third expression of the church is the Hub ("Mother") Church. These churches are larger than 200 people and tend to serve as rally points for other churches in a particular neighborhood.

A. Church Plant Expressions

1. Planting Small "House" Churches

Bunch, David, Jarvey Kneisel and Barbara Oden. *Multihousing Congregations: How to Start and Grow Christian Congregations in Multihousing Communities.* Atlanta, GA: Smith Publishing, 1991.

This is an older resource, but it is one of the only resources that provides specific ideas for those planting a church in an apartment complexes, trailer parks, or other multi-housing units.

Joel Comiskey. "Cell Church Reading List and Bibliography," accessed June 2, 2015, *http://www.joelcomiskeygroup.com/articles/churchLeaders/cellreadinglistbibliography.htm.*

Comiskey has written more than twenty-five books on cell churches (two noted below). His dissertation (available for free online) was on cell churches in Latin America and a number of his books are available in both Spanish and English. He currently teaches church planting at Tozer Seminary and consults with church plant groups interested in the cell church model. This bibliography lists 81 books he recommends on cell churches. He ranks them in the order he recommends that a cell church planter to read them.

Joel Comiskey. *2000 Years of Small Groups: A History of Cell Ministry in the Church.* Moreno, CA: CCS Publishing, 2014.

Joel Comiskey. *Biblical Foundations for the Cell-Based Church: New Testament Insights for the 21st Century Church.* Moreno, CA: CCS Publishing, 2012.

Randy Frazee and Max Lucado. *The Connecting Church 2.0: Beyond Small Groups to Authentic Community.* Grand Rapids: Zondervan, 2013.

This book is not designed exclusively for small churches, but it describes the impact a small group of committed believers can have when they focus on single geographical area. This is an important book for those wrestling with the incarnational aspect of church planting.

David Garrison. *Church Planting Movements: How God Is Redeeming a Lost World.* Midlothian, VA: WIGTake, 2004.

An important book for those seeking to understand church plant movements. This is the core textbook for TUMI's course on church plant movements.

Michael Green. *Church without Walls: A Global Examination of the Cell Church.* Waynesboro, GA: Paternoster, 2002.

Joel Comiskey ranks this as the most important book on the "Small Church." Michael Green has been writing on evangelism for more than fifty years, his early book *Evangelism in the Early Church* is a seminal book.

Larry Kreider and Floyd McClung. *Starting a House Church.* Chosen Books, 2007.

> Larry Kreider is one of the leaders of the House to House Network. This association of house churches has dozens of resources for those working with Small Church models. Several of these resources are listed below and many more can be found at *www.h2hp.com.*

Larry Kreider et al. *The Biblical Role of Elders for Today's Church: New Testament Leadership Principles for Equipping Elders.* Ephrata, PA: House To House Publication, 2015.

Larry Kreider. *House Church Networks: A Church for a New Generation.* Ephrata, PA: House to House, 2001.

Brian Sauder and Larry Kreider. *Helping You Build Cell Churches: A Comprehensive Training Manual for Pastors, Cell Leaders and Church Planters,* Updated edition. Ephrata, PA: House to House, 2000.

Scoggins, Dick. *Handbook for House Churches.* [on-line], accessed 1 December 1999, *http://genesis.acu.edu/cplant/archive/contr036*; Internet.

> This resource was designed for a network of house churches on the East Coast. The group is known as the Fellowship of Church Planters, and it is available for free at the website above.

2. Planting Community Churches

Don Allsman, Don L. Davis, and Hank Voss, eds. *Ripe for Harvest: A Guidebook for Planting Healthy Churches in the City.* Wichita, KS: TUMI Press, 2015.*

> This book is TUMI's primary textbook for the Evangel School of Church Planting. It is relevant for all expressions of the church, but is included here so as not to be missed.

Carter, Ryan, ed. *Christ the Victor Church: The Guidebook: Ancient Faith for an Urban Movement.* N.P.: CreateSpace, 2014.

The Christ the Victor (CTV) movement began in Wichita, KS and is heavily influenced by TUMI's Sacred Roots theme. This guidebook is designed for planters who are interested in planting a CTV church plant.

Davis, Don. *Focus on Reproduction*, vol. 12, 16 vols. (The Capstone Curriculum). Wichita, KS: The Urban Ministry Institute Press, 2005.*

TUMI's primary church plant course is relevant to all three church plant expressions, but is included here so as not to be missed.

Nebel, Tom. *Big Dreams in Small Places: Church Planting in Smaller Communities*. St Charles, IL: ChurchSmart Resources, 2002.

This book is focused on church planting in rural areas. It is relevant to urban church planting in that many rural areas are very poor and there are thus principles which can be gleaned by those working among the urban poor.

3. Planting Mother (Hub) Churches

Keller, Tim and J. Allen Thompson. *Church Planting Manual*. Redeemer Church Planting Center, New York, 2002.

Tim Keller and Allen Thompson have planted many urban churches over several decades. Their church plants are usually not focused on starting with the urban poor, but they are attentive to the importance of serving the poor through ministries of mercy.

Moore, Ralph. *Starting a New Church: The Church Planter's Guide to Success*. Ventura, CA: Regal Books, 2002.

Pastor Moore founded the Hope Chapel movement which has planted a number of churches among the urban poor. His book includes chapters on the importance of preaching for church planting.

Searcy, Nelson and Kerick Thomas. *Launch: Starting a New Church from Scratch*. Regal Books, 2007.

This book focuses on planting with a large nucleus from the very first service. It places much emphasis on starting large and has helpful ideas for those committed to planting a "Hub Church."

Smith, Efrem. *The Post-Black & Post-White Church: Becoming the Beloved Community in a Multi-Ethnic World.* San Francisco: Jossey-Bass Publishers, 2012.

Rev. Smith's book is specifically focused on the importance of planting a multi-ethnic church. The book describes lessons learned from church planting and will be especially helpful for those hoping to plant a large Hub Church in an urban area.

B. Associations, Denominations and Partnerships

Carter, Ryan, ed., *Christ the Victor Church: The Guidebook: Ancient Faith for an Urban Movement.* N.P.: CreateSpace, 2014.

The Christ the Victor (CTV) movement began in Wichita, KS and is heavily influenced by TUMI's Sacred Roots theme. This guidebook is designed for planters who are interested in planting a CTV church plant and provides a helpful example for other movements interested in training church planters within their movement.

Mannoia, Kevin. *Church Planting: The Next Generation.* Indianapolis, IN: Light and Life Communication, 1994.

This book is now over twenty years old, but it is still helpful for movements and denominations that are thinking through the "systems" they hope to use as their group plants churches. His emphasis on systems helps a family of churches think through how they can work together to recruit, assess, train, encourage, and empower church planters.

Romo, Oscar I. *American Mosaic Church Planting in Ethnic America.* Nashville: Broadman Press, 1993.

This book describes the church planting system in use in the early nineties in the Southern Baptist denomination.

C. Urban Church Planting

Bunch, David, Jarvey Kneisel and Barbara Oden. *Multihousing Congregations: How to Start and Grow Christian Congregations in Multihousing Communities.* Atlanta, GA: Smith Publishing, 1991.

This is an older resource, but it provides specific ideas for those planting a church in apartment complexes, trailer parks, or other multi-housing units.

Carter, Ryan, ed. *Christ the Victor Church: The Guidebook: Ancient Faith for an Urban Movement.* N.P.: CreateSpace, 2014.

As noted above, this resource is especially designed for church planters working among the urban poor.

Carter, Matt and Darrin Patrick. *For the City: Proclaiming and Living Out the Gospel.* Grand Rapids, MI: Zondervan, 2011.

This book focuses especially on church planting in urban contexts, but is not especially targeted on church planters working among the poor.

Conn, Harvie, M. ed. *Planting and Growing Urban Churches: From Dream to Reality.* Grand Rapids, MI: Baker Book House, 1996.

This is a "big picture" book on why church planting in the cities is especially important. Harvie Conn was a cross-cultural missionary for many years and has written a number of books calling the evangelical church to prioritize urban missions.

Francis, Hozell C. *Church Planting in the African American Context.* Grand Rapids, MI: Zondervan Publishing House, 2000.

This is one of several books published in the last two decades that focuses on the specific issues facing church planters targeting African-American communities.

Greenway, Roger S. and Timothy M. Monsma. *Cities: Missions' New Frontier*, 2nd Ed. Grand Rapids, MI: Baker Books, 2000.

Greenway has written a number of books on urban mission and his books offer a big picture perspective on why urban church planting needs to be a priority.

Grigg, Viv. *Cry of the Urban Poor.* MARC, a division of World Vision, 1992.

Grigg is now a professor at Azusa Pacific University teaching on urban transformational development. He has written a number of books on the urban poor. This book focuses especially on the need for church planting work among the international urban poor communities, but many of its ideas are relevant to those working with U.S. poor as well.

Hiebert, Paul G. and Eloise Hiebert Meneses. *Incarnational Ministry: Planting Churches in Band, Tribal, Peasant, and Urban Societies.* Grand Rapids, MI: Baker Publishing House, 1995.

This book is a classic and provides important sociological insight for those planting churches in urban communities, both in the United States and internationally.

Kyle, John E. ed. *Urban Mission: God's Concern for the City.* Downers Grove, IL: InterVarsity Press, 1988.

Overstreet, Don. *Sent Out: The Calling, the Character, and the Challenge of the Apostle/Missionary.* Bloomington, IN: Crossbooks, 2009.

Rev. Overstreet has helped to plant or coach more than 500 churches among the poor during the past fifty years. He currently serves as a church plant strategy coordinator in Los Angeles.

Overstreet, Don and Mark Hammond. *God's Call to the City.* Bloomington, IN: Crossbooks, 2011.

Rev. Overstreet is a strategy coordinator for the Southern Baptists and Mark Hammond has planted many African American churches in the greater Los Angeles Area. This book reflects on the implications of the book of Jonah for church planting among the poor.

Phillips, Keith. *Out of Ashes*. Los Angeles, CA: World Impact Press, 1996.

This book describes some of the philosophical and theological foundations behind World Impact's church planting strategy.

Ratliff, Joe S. and Michael J. Cox. *Church Planting in the African-American Community*. Nashville, TN: Broadman Press, 1993.

One of the first books that specifically focused on church planting in African-American contexts.

Sanders, Alvin. *Bridging the Diversity Gap: Leading Toward God's Multi-Ethnic Kingdom*. Indianapolis: Wesleyan Publishing House, 2013.

Steffen, Tom. *Passing the Baton: Church Planting That Empowers*. La Habra, CA: Center for Organizational & Ministry Development, 1997.

Steffon teaches at Biola University. This book describes church planting among the poor in an international setting, but its emphasis on empowerment of the poor from the beginning of the church planting process makes it especially relevant for those planting among the poor in the U.S.

IV. General on Church Planting

The following books and articles have proven helpful to many church planters.

Allen, Roland. *Missionary Methods, St. Paul's or Ours?* Grand Rapids, MI: William B. Eerdmans Publishing Company, 1962.

Chaney, Charles L. *Church Planting at the End of the Twentieth Century*. Wheaton, Il: Tyndale House Publishers, Inc., 1993.

Logan, Robert E. *Beyond Church Growth*. Old Tappan, New Jersey: Fleming H. Revell Co., 1989.

Malphurs, Aubrey. *Planting Growing Churches for the 21 Century: A Comprehensive Guide for New Churches and Those Desiring Renewal*, 2nd ed. Grand Rapids, MI: Baker Book House, 1998.

Mull, Marlin. *A Biblical Church Planting Manual from the Book of Acts*. Eugene, OR: Wipf and Stock Publishers, 2003.

Shenk, David W. and Ervin R. Stutzman. *Creating Communities of the Kingdom: New Testament Models of Church Planting*. Scottdale, PA: Herald Press, 1988.

Stetzer, Edward J. *Planting Missional Churches*. Nashville, TN: B&H Publishers, 2006.

Ed Stetzer and Warren Bird. "The State of Church Planting in the United States: Research Overview and Qualitative Study of Primary Church Planting Entities." (*The Leadership Network*, 2007), *www.christianitytoday.com/assets /10228.pdf*.

V. Free Church Planting Resources

Cheyney, Tom, J. David Putman and Van Sanders, eds. *Seven Steps for Planting Churches*. Alpharetta, GA: North American Mission Board, SBC, 2003.

A free resource that describes a seven-step process for church planting. It is available at *www.churchplantingvillage.net*.

Davis, Don. *www.tumi.org*.

There are hundreds of free sermons, lectures, papers, diagrams, and other resources relevant to urban church planters developed by Dr. Don Davis at *www.tumi.org*.

———. *Winning the World: Facilitating Urban Church Planting Movements* (Foundations for Ministry Series). Wichita, KS: The Urban Ministry Institute Press, 2007.

This entire course on church planting movements is available for free at *www.biblicaltraining.org*. The website *www.biblicaltraining. org* has dozens of other free seminary courses on it as well.

Chris, Richard H., compiler. *Reaching a Nation through Church Planting*. Alpharetta, GA: North American Mission Board, SBC, 2002.

This book provides a collection of essays and resources on church planting. It is available for free at *www.churchplantingvillage.net*.

Scoggins, Dick. *Handbook for House Churches.* [on-line], accessed 1 December 1999, *http://genesis.acu.edu/cplant/archive/contr036*; Internet.

A free resource on planting house churches.

Ed Stetzer and Warren Bird, "The State of Church Planting in the United States: Research Overview and Qualitative Study of Primary Church Planting Entities" (*The Leadership Network,* 2007), *www.christianitytoday.com/assets /10228.pdf.*

This forty-page research report provides one of the most important big picture surveys of church planting in the United States currently available.

Gary Teja and John Wagenveld, eds. *Planting Healthy Churches.* Sauk Village, IL: Multiplication Network Ministries, 2015.

Free downloadable resource for students interested in church planting; PowerPoint and other teaching resources are also available.

VI. Women Church Planting

It can be difficult to find resources designed to support women involved in church planting. The following resources are either by or about women involved with church planting.

Allen, Tricia. "Single Church Planter: Singles Must Step Up to Lead." *Wesleyan Life* 6 (Summer 2011): 6-7.

Chilcote, Paul Wesley. "Lessons from the 'Society Planting': Paradigm of Early Methodist Women: 2012 AETE Presidential Address." *Witness: Journal of the Academy for Evangelism in Theological Education* 27 (2013):5–30.

Emmanuel Gospel Center. "The Unsolved Leadership Challenge: A Report on Greater Boston Church Planters and What They Believe about Women in Leadership," October 2014, *http://egc. org/sites/egc.org/files/The%20Unsolved%20Leadership%20 Challenge_Church%20Planters%20and%20Women%20in%20 Leadership_0.pdf.*

Dale, Felicity. *Getting Started: A Practical Guide to House Church Planting*. Karis Publishing, Inc., 2003.

Hamp, Angie. *Confessions of a Church Planter's Wife: Coming Clean about the Dirty Side of Church Planting*. N.P.: Create Space, 2011.

Hoover, Christine. *The Church Planting Wife: Help and Hope for Her Heart*. Chicago: Moody Publishers, 2013.

————. *Partners in Planting: Help and Encouragement for Church Planting Wives*. An ebook available at "Grace Covers Me." *www. gracecoversme.com*. 2014.

Thomas, Shari. *The Primary Sources of Stress and Satisfaction among PCA Church Planting Spouses*. Atlanta: Mission to North America, 2005.

Wilson, Linda. "Issues for Women in Church Planting." *Evangelical Missions Quarterly* 39, no.3 (July 2003): 362–366.

Reddin, Opal. *Planting Churches That Grow*. Springfield, MO: Central Bible College Press, 1990.

VII. Specialized Bibliographies

Dr. Don L. Davis, ed. *Planting Churches among the City's Poor: An Anthology of Urban Church Planting Resources*. Wichita, KS: The Urban Ministry Institute Press, 2015. 2 Volumes.*

Both volumes of the anthology include a five-page bibliography of resources especially relevant for urban church planters.

Joel Comiskey, "Cell Church Reading List and Bibliography," accessed June 2, 2015, *http://www.joelcomiskeygroup.com/articles/ churchLeaders/cellreadinglistbibliography.htm*.

Comiskey has written more than twenty-five books on cell churches. His doctoral research was on cell churches in Latin America and a number of his books are available in both Spanish and English. He currently teaches church planting at Tozer Seminary and consults with church plant groups interested in the cell church model. This bibliography lists eighty-one books he recommends on cell churches. They are ranked by him in the order that he would recommend a cell church planter to read them.

Ed Stetzer, "Church Planting Bibliography," *The Exchange*, April 20, 2009, *http://www.christianitytoday.com/edstetzer*.

This free online bibliography is an annotated list of seventy books related to church planting in North America. The content of each book is briefly summarized and Stetzer usually provides a one or two sentence evaluation of the books merits for church planters. Seven of the seventy books (10%) have some relevancy to urban church planting, although none are specifically concerned with the challenge of planting churches among the urban poor in North America. Two of the seventy books are written by women.

Hank Voss, "A Select Bibliography of Works by Rev. Dr. Don L. Davis," in *Black and Human: Rediscovering King as a Resource for Black Theology and Ethics*, ed. Don L. Davis. Wichita, KS: TUMI Press, 2015, pp. 295–310.

This bibliography covers more than 100 resources developed by Dr. Don Davis relevant to those involved with urban church planting and cross cultural missions.

APPENDIX 36

Handing Down the Apostolic Deposit:
Passing Down the Story through Discipleship and Tradition

Rev. Dr. Don L. Davis

Guard the Good Deposit

Follow the pattern of the sound words that you have heard from me, in the faith and love that are in Christ Jesus. By the Holy Spirit who dwells within us, guard the good deposit entrusted to you.
~ 2 Tim. 1.13-14

You, however, have followed my teaching, my conduct, my aim in life, my faith, my patience, my love, my steadfastness, my persecutions and sufferings that happened to me at Antioch, at Iconium, and at Lystra—which persecutions I endured; yet from them all the Lord rescued me.
~ 2 Tim. 3.10-11

Protect the Entrusted Story

O Timothy, guard the deposit entrusted to you. Avoid the irreverent babble and contradictions of what is falsely called "knowledge"
~1 Tim. 6.20

Now we command you, brothers, in the name of our Lord Jesus Christ, that you keep away from any brother who is walking in idleness and not in accord with the tradition that you received from us.
~ 2 Thess. 3.6

Paul

Timothy and Many Witnesses

The Same Commit Thou to Faithful Men

Who Shall Be Able to Teach Others Also

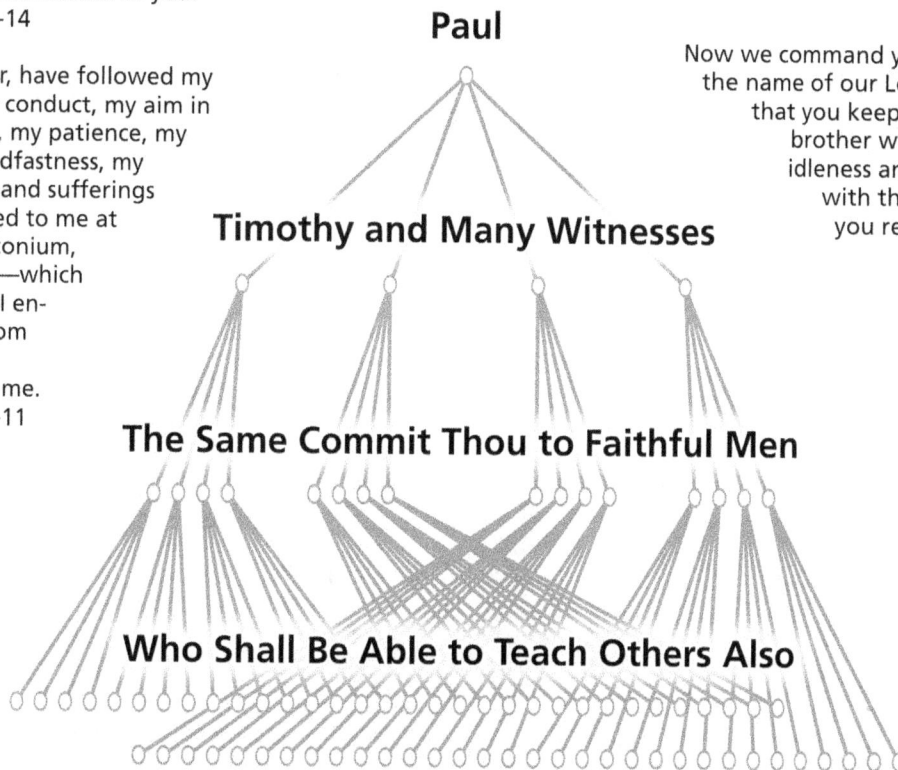

2 Tim. 2.2 (ESV) – And what you have heard from me in the presence of many witnesses entrust to faithful men who will be able to teach others also.

The key to multiplying disciples is equipping others with the very story, truths, practices, and traditions which the apostles handed down to their faithful disciples, who in obedience to Christ passed them down through the generations, even to us.

What is the center of this tradition? It is the story of God's saving actions in Christ – his coming, incarnation, passion, crucifixion, burial, resurrection, ascension, session, and second Coming. They were eyewitnesses of his Majesty, and commanded his church to walk worthy of their calling, testifying in word and deed of the hope of his return. To disciple is to ground people in this Story of God in Christ in the midst of Christian assembly, expressed in a shared spirituality and through a common identity – in worship, faith, service, and witness.

www.ingramcontent.com/pod-product-compliance
Lightning Source LLC
Chambersburg PA
CBHW081641040426

42449CB00015B/3414